Unwrapping the Gifts

of

Recovery

UNWRAPPING THE GIFTS

OF

RECOVERY

Effective Tools

for Chemical Dependency Counseling

H. Leroy Thompson

ISBN 13: 9781494777487
ISBN 10: 1494777487

Printed in the United States of America

Library of Congress Control Number: 2014900614
CreateSpace Independent Publishing Platform
North Charleston, South Carolina

To those who gave me the opportunity to journey with them through their time of struggling, searching, discovering, and recovering.

CONTENTS

PREFACE

This book is a collection of effective tools that I discovered through many years as pastoral counselor, a chemical dependency (CD) family counselor, and an administrator of a hospital-based chemical dependency unit (CDU). My educational background and counselor training is included at the back of this book. In the acknowledgments, you will learn more about my training.

I have been a trainer/counseling supervisor for state agencies, hospitals, and nonprofit organizations and an Employee Assistance Program consultant to businesses. In retirement, I continue to provide training and consultation to different programs when I have the opportunity and time.

The title, *Unwrapping the Gifts of Recovery: Effective Tools for Chemical Dependency Counseling,* reflects the broad perspective of resources that I have acquired through years of working in the field of CD.

I have a deep appreciation for those who have dedicated their lives to help individuals and families battling the trials and tribulations of this complex disease. We CD professionals are rewarded by witnessing the transformation of addicted persons as they discover the recovery process and celebrate sobriety. We have the opportunity to share in opening the gifts of recovery, and we have the privilege of walking beside each one who has begun this journey. The French historian and philosopher Voltaire wrote, "God gave us the gift of life; it is up to us to give ourselves the gift of living well."[1]

Counseling is a rewarding profession. The satisfaction of observing change in another person is a "natural high." The quality of your counseling will be equal to the knowledge and professional training you receive.

This book is presented as a resource for your counseling with the chemically dependent. There is a balance between step-by-step guides for each tool and the rationale for applying them to CD counseling. The tools offered appear to be focused on individual clients, but they are best used in a therapy group. Active counseling of the chemically dependent should happen within a group of peers, co-clients, and patients (see "The Value of Group Therapy").

You may find yourself wondering, debating, or reexamining your approach to counseling as you study these approaches. You could even catch yourself doubting the efficacy of what you read. This is a natural progression for anyone willing to change and grow. I recall Richard Bandler, one of the pioneers of Neuro-Linguistic Programming (NLP), stating,

> *"If you can make something new fit into what you already know, you will learn nothing from it, and nothing will change in your behavior. You will only have a comfortable feeling of understanding, a complacency that will keep you from learning anything new."[2]*

There is an inherent risk in disclosing one's personal philosophical and experiential background. I am exposing my biases, beliefs, and values. I hope you will integrate what is valuable to you and expand your skill base. I challenge you to experiment with the concepts that are more troublesome for you before discounting or discarding them.

This book is not a primer, but it reviews fundamental principles and practices of counseling modalities and the valuable tools that I have found effective. Read the notes and bibliography for more detailed information regarding each tool presented. I have presumed that you have some basic knowledge of and training in CD, human development, behavioral science, and general counseling theory. At the same time, there are many professionals who do not know or use these tools. I have trained in outpatient and inpatient programs over the years; each time these tools have been introduced, the counselors were amazed at their results.

This book does not present new concepts or tools. I have no interest in attempting to improve these tools or introduce original ones. My intent is to apply the counseling tools to CD and review the core principles essential to effective CD counseling.

My professional education has been influenced by teachings that include Transactional Analysis (TA), Gestalt therapy, NLP (not a therapy model), Reality therapy, Adlerian theory, and other counseling models. I have input from former trainees and counselors of the proven effectiveness of these integrated tools with their clients. I have used every one of these tools when counseling chemically dependent patients and their families. Your training and experience can be coupled with the tools.

Keep in mind the "micro" and "macro" perceptions regarding any information offered. Maintain symmetry between macroscopic and microscopic observations when interacting with those you counsel. A macroscopic vision encompasses your whole biopsychosocial history, which affects the way you view and experience everything. A macroscopic activity operates with a panoramic scope; you see the whole rather than the parts.

On the other hand, microscopic vision is focused and localized. This view notices the "trees within the forest." Skilled counselors learn to keep centered on the immediate and connect the present to past and future events. I concentrate on guiding you to hone your microscopic counseling skills.

Popular bestselling author Stephen Covey discovered this truth, but he stated it differently:

"I became particularly interested in how perceptions are formed, how they govern the way we see, and how the way we see governs how we behave. This led me to a study of expectancy theory and self-fulfilling prophecies or the 'Pygmalion effect,' and to a realization of how deeply imbedded our perceptions are. It taught me that we must look at the lens through which we see the world, as well as at the world we see, and that the lens itself shapes how we interpret the world."[3]

Let me clarify another point before jumping into the "meat" of this book. I use the terms *counselor* and *counseling* throughout. They are functional definitions and not clinical dynamics. I am aware of the clinical distinctions between *counseling* and *therapy*. Not all counselors are therapists, but all therapists are counselors. Therapy technically involves methods for change, and counseling is a guiding activity. A professional therapist typically has an educational degree coupled with intense, clinical training and supervision and some type of certification or licensure. A professional counselor will have the educational and certification qualifications and a background of practical training. While counselors are not therapists in the literal or legal sense, they can be change agents in the counseling process.

I have written this book for both counselors and therapists. You can apply these teachings in a way that augments your definitive training and competence.

You can scan this book quickly due to its length—it can be a swift reference source, or you can intentionally study it. If you choose to study it, plan to spend time *internalizing* the tools. Read slowly and experiment. Practice what you read. Learn what you practice. Apply what you learn.

Your counseling proficiency will be enhanced as you test the tools. Your enjoyment will be matched by the time and energy you invest in developing personally and professionally. My professional journey has been enriched by those mentors and patients who have graced my life. I have learned more than I can ever give. I wish for you the same.

You will notice throughout the book that I interchange the male and female pronouns. I am sensitive to gender exclusivity and have chosen to remain faithful to my philosophical focus. I have five grown daughters and no sons, so I could have no other approach.

H. Leroy Thompson
December 30, 2013

Acknowledgments

I have been enriched and blessed through my professional career. There is a long list of mentors, trainers, professors, supervisors, and bosses who influenced my development as a counselor, trainer, instructor, administrator, and collaborator. I received a wide education including extensive reading in diverse fields.

Dr. Harry Boyd, PhD, clinical psychologist, introduced, trained, and supervised my clinical training in TA and Gestalt therapy through an institute he founded, the Midwest Institute for TA and Gestalt Therapy. His keen mind and wit challenged me to stay focused on "games," "ego states," corresponding "contaminations," "life scripts," "escape hatches," and much more. I acquired a profound indebtedness and understanding that TA was neither a "pop psychology" nor a momentary trend. This theory has a proven history and endures as a vital modality for counselors and psychotherapists.[4]

The late Don Blackerby, PhD, educator and psychologist, ran his own consulting company, Success Skills, Inc. He inspired many people and specialized in applying NLP to the learning process, helping struggling students of all ages. His book, *Rediscover the Joy of Learning*, was published in three languages and sold worldwide.

Don and I became friends and mutually decided to exchange knowledge and training. He participated in a clinical training program for CD counselors that I conducted at HCA Presbyterian Hospital, and Don provided me training in NLP. We worked together to interface NLP with addiction counseling and were pleased by some significant results.

Don provided in-service training for the hospital clinical staff and the counselors in the adolescent unit. He was helpful in reviewing the data in this book related to NLP theory.

The late Vernon Enlow, PhD, clinical psychologist, was instrumental in guiding me in family systems through his familiarity with the works of Alfred Adler, Carl Rogers, Virginia Satir, and others. He invited me to workshops that he sponsored where he brought in well-known family therapy practitioners and authorities. He taught me about adolescent development and how to be effective in counseling adolescents. Vernon conducted effective in-service training for our clinical staff in the adolescent CD unit.

The late Dr. Boyd Lester, MD, psychiatrist and professor of psychiatry at Oklahoma University Medical School, spent years in research and teaching in the area of alcoholism and alcohol abuse. During his time in private practice, he was the hospital consulting psychiatrist for our treatment program. He was a wonderful asset to our counseling and nursing staff. His sense of humor and down-to-earth approach to therapy presented a dynamic model for working with the chemically dependent and their families.

I had the added opportunity of attending weekly group sessions with other CD counselors who were receiving training and supervision from Dr. Lester. He grounded us in the distinctions between "addiction" counseling and psychotherapy.

There are numerous others, too many to list, who were influential in my growth as a pastoral counselor, CD counselor, family counselor (families with a chemically dependent member), and administrator of inpatient and outpatient treatment services. My gratitude to each one cannot be adequately expressed in words.

INTRODUCTION

Your philosophy regarding human personality and behavior is the foundation of your counseling approach. Do you believe in the positive potential of human beings, or are you suspicious of hidden motives? When your client, or anyone else you know, appears hesitant to change, do you interpret this as an "unhealthy resistance to counseling"? Do you tend to doubt that others have a sincere desire to transform when they continue using the same old behaviors?

Stephen Covey learned for himself how the "Pygmalion effect" shaped human interaction. Some consider it a negative condition. They hold to the idea that a person falls in love with the creation of his mind. Others carelessly apply this tendency to therapists who assume that they are to treat their clients as children since they have limited ego-strength to do otherwise. Still more argue that this is a self-fulfilling prophecy, and what you expect is most likely to happen. Confusing, isn't it?

Despite the definition or term, I am convinced that every person has a *tropistic principle*. This theory maintains that in every living organism, from the simplest to the most complex, there is an innate movement toward the power or source that keeps it alive. The dynamic is identical for a flower growing toward the light or a human being searching for wholeness. According to renowned psychologist Abraham Maslow, humans are created to actualize their potential. His classic theory on the "hierarchy of needs" remains valid for understanding motivation and personal development.

Dr. Jean Houston was a major influence on my beliefs regarding human nature and development. A prime mover in the "human potential movement," her lectures, workshops, and numerous books nurtured my soul and exploded my mind. She reinforced the healing art within each of us.

> *"Indeed, it has been shown that it is possible, through conscious directed thought, to control the firing of a single motor neuron. With subtly developed body awareness, it is possible for the individual to become the conscious orchestrator of health. We can no longer escape the understanding that psyche and soma are inextricably woven together."*[5]

As human beings, unlike other living organisms such as plants and trees, we have the unique capacity to interrupt our growth. We have an *operational will* to refuse this "living" tendency. We can say, "No!" No other form of life has this gift (or is it a curse?). This view is underscored by the late, noted author Dr. Muriel James. I participated in a workshop in which she was asked, "How does a person change"? She replied, "That's the wrong question! The proper question is how you *stop* yourself from changing."

I work with the counseling axiom that truth and change are both within and beyond the client. I do not hold a magical wand for revelation or transformation, much less sobriety and recovery.

Hippocrates, the great Greek physician who gave the art of medicine the Hippocratic Oath, believed that no physician heals. He argued that a physician aids the human body in connecting with the transcendent healing process. Doctors do not perform miracles. The healing miracle is possible because the tropistic functions of life are present. His seminal work, *The Complicated Body,* is considered the groundwork for what physicians still believe. He wrote it during his twenty years in prison.

"Nevertheless, through observation, touch, prognosis, and gentle patient treatment, Hippocrates concluded and taught basics such as, 'Natural forces within us are the true healers of disease,' and 'Walking is man's best medicine.' So powerful was his argument and his successful results with patients that he succeeded in separating the discipline of medicine from religion and philosophy with his persevering insistence that disease was not a punishment inflicted by the gods, but largely the product of environmental factors, genetics, and/or bad diet and unwise or unfortunate living habits and conditions."[5]

My credo is that the nature of God, the higher power of our living process, has created us with a genetic makeup for natural healing. The 12 Steps of Alcoholics Anonymous (AA) are built on this foundation as Bill Wilson and Dr. Bob Smith conceived it. However, they both admitted that the alcoholic cannot "self-will" his way to sobriety without the guidance of his higher power.

My experience indicates that most helping professions operate from this principle of natural healing, but do not mistake this as a Mary Baker Eddy (Christian Science) philosophy of healing where no physician is considered necessary in the cure of an illness except God alone. Even those who are deluded by omnipotence ultimately must concede how powerless they are over persons and events. I ought to temper this statement to say that "power addicts" are reluctant to make this concession, but I believe they do so when their desired outcomes never materialize. There is hope when any addict discovers how his addiction sabotages growth and fulfillment and comes to accept the power within and without to change.

If your philosophy does not hold firmly to an "actualizing" and "transcending" theory, I wonder about your motive for being in the counseling profession. Burnout is imminent. I will be bold and suggest that you consider changing your philosophy or changing your profession.

Healing and change happen. People do become healthy. Counseling and therapy help us reconnect to ever-present healing forces, but counseling and therapy never change anyone. The chemically dependent are not cured, but they can know healthy options for living sober, and they can reap the rewards of recovery. This is what I call healing: one of several gifts of recovery.

CHAPTER 1

THE CONTEXT OF COUNSELING WITH THE CHEMICALLY DEPENDENT

It is essential to restate the context of CD counseling within the medical model for diagnosing and treating this "disease." This is the implied approach used throughout this book. I am aware of the social model that argues for the learned behavioral patterns manifested by compulsive disorders. Cian Kerrisk a thoughtful psychotherapist makes a distinction between the disease and the harm reduction models:

"In contrast to the disease model, the harm reduction model espouses the belief that people with previous alcohol problems can maintain minimal substance use and drink/drug socially in a controlled manner (Valliant, 1996, cited Emmenkamp & Vedel, 2006). Such views are based on the premise that although abstinence is necessary in some cases, addiction is treatable. Harm reduction also relates

to reducing risky behaviours associated with use and is epitomised by needle exchange programmes (ADIO, 2010) and the Community Alcohol and Drug Service methadone programme (CADS, 2010)."[7]

Conversely, in a large hospital CD unit, our physicians and professional staff provided treatment using the medical model, and the efficacy of our treatment was evaluated by a nationally recognized agency that performed outcome studies of our patients and families. Comparative studies were conducted relative to other treatment programs in the United States. The hospital contracted with a chemical addiction treatment outcome registry, and this organization reported a recidivism rate of 12 percent in a two-year follow-up survey. This study included adult and adolescent patients.

Our treatment philosophy was holistic in all of our treatment approaches, which included Alcoholics Anonymous (AA) and Narcotics Anonymous (NA) 12 Step groups. We based our treatment on a firm family-oriented structure. The clinical and professional staff were trained and certified in various approaches for treating our patients and family members.

In 1956, the American Medical Association declared that alcoholism was an illness. In 1968, the definition was expanded:

"Alcoholism is an illness characterized by preoccupation with alcohol and loss of control over its consumption such as to lead usually to intoxication if drinking is begun; by chronicity; by progression; and by tendency toward relapse. It is typically associated with

physical disability and impaired emotional, occupational, and/or social adjustments as a direct consequence of persistent and excessive use of alcohol."[8]

The Diagnostic and Statistical Manual of Mental Disorders (DSM) does not use the word *addiction*. *Substance use disorder* is the classification, and it is not considered a "mental disorder." The criteria are as follows:

"When an individual persists in use of alcohol or other drugs despite problems related to use of the substance, substance dependence may be diagnosed. Compulsive and repetitive use may result in tolerance to the effect of the drug and withdrawal symptoms when use is reduced or stopped. The DSM-V states... 'Criteria are provided for substance use disorder, accompanied by criteria for intoxication, withdrawal, substance/medication-induced disorders, and unspecified substance-induced disorders, where relevant.'"[9]

The definitions by the American Medical Association (AMA) and the DSM-IV/DSM-V underscore the distinct characteristics of the chemically dependent. Cooperative actions between the medical professions and behavioral scientists are showing the complex nature of chemical dependence, thus affirming an inclusive approach to the problem. I applaud this encompassing world view.

The practical tools you will discover in this book can only be applied once a clear diagnosis and a well-defined treatment plan have been completed with the assistance of your client. The treatment plan is for the chemically dependent, not for you. You are guiding the process of treatment and not controlling it.

The following description is vital to using each tool presented here within a treatment plan or in the process of establishing a treatment contract with your client. A mental health service says:

> *"The good treatment plan is a comprehensive set of tools and strategies that address the client's identifiable strengths as well as her or his problems and deficits. It presents an approach for sequencing resources and activities, and identifies benchmarks of progress to guide evaluation."*[10]

AN OVERVIEW OF ADDICTION COUNSELING IN CONTRAST TO PSYCHOTHERAPY

There are many modalities for counseling the chemically dependent such as brief therapy, reality therapy, cognitive therapy, and behavioral modification. As stated previously, there are successful counseling modalities that can be effective with your chemically dependent client. Each person you counsel will be more amenable and responsive to one particular concept. Do not limit yourself to using one protocol.

Addiction counseling is predicated on understanding that the CD is the primary focus of treatment, and until an addict has established a basic acceptance and practice of abstinence, no treatment will advance. Before abstinence can be attained, you must ask your medical staff or medical director if the patient has been fully detoxed. In Presbyterian hospital, we did not place a patient in group therapy until she was capable of functioning without her chemical of choice. The staff used the pre-counseling period for conducting an assessment, developing a bio-psychosocial history and psychological testing, and obtaining a psychiatric evaluation of possible dual disorders, especially those that required maintenance medications for daily functioning.

Boyd Lester, MD, was the consulting psychiatrist for our hospital. He informed our treatment team that 10–20 percent (perhaps more) of patients had dual disorders and would require constant observation and supervision of their medications. Dr. Lester acknowledged that it was common for the chemically dependent patient's drug-use history to mask or mimic mental disorders. The medical staff was assigned the task of determining the precipitating factors, but the psychiatrist ascertained whether abstinence of these focal medications was not viable and could impede treatment related to dependence on alcohol, cocaine, methamphetamine, heroin, marijuana, etc. He gave another warning that 80–90 percent of patients admitted to psychiatric units had primary psychological disorders and approximately 10–20 percent had a dual diagnosis of secondary CD. It was assumed that some patients would have to be transferred to the proper treatment setting for care.

If you are in private practice, I strongly advise you to never set a goal of abstinence without doing a medical assessment and physical on your client. It is dangerous to have a chemically dependent client stop "cold turkey." Withdrawal, with all of its reactionary symptoms, can be fatal without the proper medical supervision.

Addiction counseling does not require that a counselor be a recovering addict. You can be effective as long as you have thorough training in the field. I learned this valuable lesson when I attended an intensive training workshop at the Johnson Institute of Minnesota, which has a fifty-year history of promoting the power and possibility of recovery from alcoholism and other drugs. My experience happened more than forty years ago, but it provided a lasting appreciation for the dynamics of addiction treatment. The "Minnesota Model" was adopted across this nation in many medical facilities with outpatient services. Treatment was provided in a CDU rather than a mental health or psychiatric unit. Treatment outcomes began to validate the efficacy of the model. Chemical dependency is a primary disease, and it requires the skills of trained and certified addiction counselors. Much of my training was developed in the process of becoming certified as a chemical dependency counselor (CDC) at the state, national, and international levels.

One primary distinction between CD counseling and traditional psychotherapy is clarified as follows:

"Psychotherapy, particularly of the psychoanalytic variety, has a tarnished reputation as a treatment for alcohol dependence. Psychoanalysts and psycho-dynamically oriented psychotherapists theorized that alcoholism was a symptom of an underlying conflict

and that gaining insight into the origin and nature of the conflict would provide a 'cure' of the alcohol dependence. Treatment of alcohol dependent patients using this paradigm was rarely effective in producing alcohol abstinence, and many patients remained in psychotherapy for years while the severity of their alcoholism progressed."[11]

I do not accept the notion there is a chasm separating the fields of CD and psychotherapy. No doubt there are professionals who remain territorial or whose biases prevent them from cooperating, much less collaborating, in bringing wholeness to anyone suffering from addictive disorders and/or mental maladies. My counseling begins with the chemically dependent, focusing on her chemical obsessions *first*. Once we have worked through the process to sobriety and recovery, she can address her underlying history of distress, dysfunction, and despair.

You will find in this material that I have incorporated a fairly holistic set of practical tools for guiding your counseling practices. The bibliography will complement and expand your knowledge.

The Need for an Assessment

How do you know whether your client is an "abuser" or drug dependent? Without a comprehensive assessment, you cannot proceed with any type of treatment. The assessment determines the level of care needed for your client.

Screening and assessment tools include the Alcohol Use Disorders Identification Test (AUDIT), the Brief Michigan

Alcoholism Screening Test (BMAST), and the Addiction Severity Index (ASI). The assessment that I found the most proficient and comprehensive, based on clinical criteria, is the one our hospital used twenty-five years ago, and it continues to be the best resource. It is the instrument developed by Norman G. Hoffmann, PhD, clinical psychologist and president of Evince Assessment: the SUDDS-5 (Substance Use Disorder Diagnostic Schedule-5). According to Dr. Hoffmann, the assessment provides the following:

- *"It is an intake diagnostic tool for substance-related disorders.*
- *It is ideal for use in case management, such as oversight, following positive drug tests for safety-sensitive workers.*
- *It is helpful in situations where litigation or challenges to findings might be involved.*
- *It is excellent for developing court testimony or any situation where detailed objective documentation is required.*
- *It can be completed in a single session or in segments over multiple sessions without losing the context of previous responses.*
- *It collects prognostic information relevant to American Society of Addiction Medicine criteria.*
- *The respondent sign-off provides an option to have individuals attest to the accuracy of the information provided.*

    The SUDDS-5 is a comprehensive interview that provides documentation of substance-specific diagnoses based on the DSM-5.

This 35 to 45-minute interview covers both current and lifetime indications of substance use disorders. It also screens for current and past indications of depression and anxiety disorders.

Internal consistency reliability coefficients for individual substances range from .90 to .98.

This instrument provides information compatible with ASAM criteria for treatment planning and placement."[12]

This assessment has proven to be an important instrument. It validates multiple factors when determining a diagnosis of CD. Whomever you use for the assessment, be sure that the data you are collecting is wide ranging and reliable. Do not initiate counseling until you have a sufficient basis for providing treatment or making a placement to an outpatient or inpatient environment.

THE VALUE OF GROUP THERAPY

You most likely have gotten trapped while working with your client through all the manipulations and fabrications. This is a common occurrence for the average CD counselor. Assessments must include information from a family member or significant other. Sessions with only the addict should earn "hazard pay." After a one-on-one session, you might well question your sanity about wanting to work in this field. I have had my moments!

Group therapy has been a core trait of alcohol and other drug-dependency treatments for several decades, and it has proven to be effective. Chemical dependency is a systemic illness, and most every interfacing system in an addict's life has been affected. Group counseling by its very structure places your client in a world of interactions and quickly reveals interpersonal issues. Group counseling is not a 12 Step activity. Groups have specific functions, goals, and objectives. Here are some reasons why you should consider doing groups (if you are not currently engaged in them).

Group therapy offers recovering addicts the assistance and experience of peers on a related path; it offers them the hope that recovery is possible by observing others, thus creating a communal or even familial feeling of support and less social isolation.

The group dynamic provides feedback from a variety of viewpoints, facilitating your client's ability to attain greater self-awareness and understand how her behavior impacts others.

A group helps define structure, discipline, and limits for each member of the group while permitting pragmatic learning and exchange of realistic facts about drug use and the damaging effects on one's family and other close relationships. A context for honesty is established, and clients find it difficult to con you, especially those who are experts in the art of conning.

Group support provides a safe environment for experimenting with new behaviors. As the counselor, you can give directives to your client to explore fresh ways of thinking and behaving by getting encouragement and support from her peers. You also have the opportunity to address illusions, myths, and distorted perceptions resulting from her addiction.

Group participation requires an openness to be confronted and to work through conflict issues. What better setting for learning to cope with relationship problems that have evolved as by-products of addiction? This is a way to discover and practice reconciling habits regarding problems in the family and at work.

I am a strong advocate for gender-specific groups for issues unique to gender identity. Multicultural groups for understanding and coping with racial, ethnic, and minority world views that are in conflict with our diverse society are also needed. This book does not explore the dynamics of these various groups. There are many good resources found on the Internet, and numerous books are available through publishers.

CHAPTER 2

ESTABLISHING THE COUNSELING RELATIONSHIP

You may have natural instincts for relating to other people and feel comfortable in your role as a counselor. Perhaps you feel confident in your ability to create a relationship with a new client. You most likely have met clients with whom you had difficulty forming a working connection no matter how exceptional you may have felt. The following exercises are offered as a means for making a successful beginning. My introduction to counseling did not provide this information. I learned it much later in my career when I received training in NLP.

The next set of tools relates to the principles of reframing, which is discussed in chapter 6.

BUILDING RAPPORT

Rapport is the ability to interact with another person and gain his trust. It allows you to understand him. It is the ability to move from your map of reality to his and know that you are communicating.[13]

Communication will only be as effective as the quality of your rapport. This means forming a common bond through linking your internal map with his world view. You will find that concentrating on the similarities and not the differences between you will hasten rapport.

You have not attained rapport when you claim to understand your client. Rapport occurs at the moment that your client feels you understand him. Have you ever had someone tell you in an omnipotent manner, "I know you better than you think I do"? What pomposity and naiveté! Be on the alert for such assumptions when interacting with others, especially those you counsel. Rapport is an acknowledgment of *mutual* understanding, not mind reading. You can achieve rapport by using the following two key transactions.

1. **Pacing**

   Pacing is the subtle process of mirroring or matching a person's communication patterns. This does not mean that you mimic every word or movement, for this is "aping," not pacing. You want to be sensitive and responsive to your client's word framing and analogical cuing. Proactive avenues for accomplishing pacing include the following.

   Matching Predicates

   Predicates are "process" words that represent or reference a person's internal experiences through the visual, auditory (tonal), and kinesthetic modalities. Listen to the words your client uses while describing what he sees, hears, or feels when sharing about his life.

Replay what your client says by using his "frames of reference." Don't inappropriately mix or alter the frame(s). You won't need to repeat the exact words that you heard, but be consistent in representing your understanding of what he said, for example:

Client: "I am feeling anxious about being here. My stomach is in knots, and I sense an urge to run."

Counselor: "So you're feeling scared and physically tense now?"

The kinesthetic predicates are evident in this client's disclosure. Make your response match the word frames within the client's "internal map" without parroting him.

Matching Analogical Activity

The word *analogical* refers to the nonverbal patterns of response that parallel the verbal expressions of the person's experience. These are activities such as the voice tone, gestures, breathing, posture, weight shifts, etc. An *analog* is any form of output exclusive of word-symbols. They indicate what the word represents to your client.

Observe your client's physical movements, the speed of his speech, his breathing (shallow or deep), and his body posture (crossed legs and arms). Mirror the analogical patterns of the client as a way of "entering his infrastructure" of meaning. This is a sophisticated style of "walking in another person's shoes."

Matching Accessing Cues

Accessing cues are eye movements that indicate how the client retrieves thoughts and experiences stored in the brain. These are the more subtle motions that require keen observation skills, and they are also more difficult to match. Watch for the following:

a. Visual remembered—upper left

b. Visual constructed—upper right

c. Auditory remembered—level left

d. Auditory constructed—level right

e. Auditory digital—down and left

f. Kinesthetic—down and right (this scheme is transposed for some left-handed people, so always check for it)

Use these accessing cues for reinforcing your understanding of a client's frame of reference or representational system. Match or mirror these rarely unless doing so would have an impact on the client.

Matching Beliefs and Values

Be aware of any beliefs and values your client presents during your initial conversations. Restating the belief or value with the same analogical responses of your client is perhaps the most powerful rapport-building exercise you can do. In essence, you have accepted his model of the world without agreeing.

2. Leading

Leading is the second key function in developing rapport with your client. Leading begins only after you have successfully matched your client's frame of reference. As you create an effective pacing link, you can start influencing the client's response to you. The objective is to have him subconsciously "pace" your communication patterns. The importance of leading (or guiding) is to help him relax with you and gain a new perspective.

In leading or pacing, a person's response is more important than the content. Rapport building centers on *how* he speaks rather than *what* he says. Through this process, you and your client can discover the hidden operations that sustain his life.

You will usually know that rapport is satisfactorily developed by positive responses. He will nod his head in agreement or verbally acknowledge a sense of your understanding. If he appears confused, bewildered, or resistive, these indicate that you have not built rapport.

Your client presents analogical cues that offer additional verification of rapport. His body is more relaxed, his arms and legs are more open (not tightly crossed), his eyes are focused (not constricted), his breathing is deep (not shallow), and his voice is more resonant (not hollow). There is a generalized receptivity to you and the counseling environment. You feel that you are *blending* with your client instead of being a detached observer. The analogical reactions will be consistent with your shared sense of comfort.

EFFECTIVE COUNSELING REQUIRES THE POWERFUL Ps

A positive response to counseling and therapeutic changes flows through the path of trust. Rapport is pivotal in the counseling process, especially in relation to trust, yet another set of tools underlies and reinforces rapport building. Claude Steiner, Ph.D., author and trainer on Transactional Analysis (TA) in one of his abstracts wrote the following:

> *"The three operations of the process of Transactional Analysis are permission, protection and potency. Permission to change unwanted behaviors, protection from the Critical Parent and other influences that will resist or counteract the desired changes, and potency-the transactional analyst's information, skills and personal support and investment in the process."*[14]

These three operations are typically referred to as the "Powerful Ps."

Potency

Potency is the ability to establish limits and boundaries with a client without getting into a "power struggle." As the counselor, you are the guiding power during the counseling session, yet you never usurp the power of the client. You want to avoid control/power struggle issues. You should "bail out" whenever you find yourself in this situation. This is one way to exercise your potency through the wise choice of eluding the control issue.

Potency is the healthy kind of power that is secure in setting personal and professional limits without exceeding them. Control is usually a problem when you face a sense of inadequacy or impotency, and your power seems to be slipping away. You encounter impotency when giving your power and energy away. Many a counselor has burned out because he spent his energy trying to fix others.

A counselor's potency promotes the client's ability to tap into his energy and power source. Initially, this will occur through the classic mechanism of transference. In psychoanalytic therapy, the client's thoughts, feelings, and desires are projected onto the therapist. The client reacts to the therapist as though he was a parent figure or significant other from the past. Potency, in the counseling context, is engaging transference as a mobilizing power for therapeutic change. During the early stages of counseling, outside the client's awareness, you will be acting as a surrogate, so power struggles are inevitable. Your client's "inner child" (Child ego state defined in Transactional Analysis) turns to the parent (counselor) for guidance.

Permission

Another major task you have is encouraging your client to explore new behaviors and feelings. He is given permission to test discoveries without violating values, beliefs, or violations that could trigger guilt or shame.

You grant permission by saying something like, "It's okay to feel or think whatever you're experiencing." At that moment, you give your client the unavailable "parental" permission that allows him to "own" his feelings, thoughts, behaviors, and attitudes. He probably has no internal consent to make this happen. He is likely reacting to an inner, controlling parent who disdains such possibilities. Your support and encouragement will provide the nurturing atmosphere needed for making trial runs with these novel ideas. You will be pleased at how your potency as a counselor will be confirmed when your client takes these risks.

Be prudent, and advise your client that you give permission only for the counseling sessions. He needs to rely on your directives until he has enough skills to function independently. Throughout counseling, your client should be developing these essential resources, but initially, the therapeutic transference and permission are interwoven through your nurturing support.

Protection

It is normal for anyone to have some fear of change and the unknown. At the beginning, the client is uncertain about therapy and how to internalize healthy boundaries for self-protection. The addictive person in particular is living in a personal and interpersonal world gone out of control. A deluded sense of control is assumed to be the power of self-management. Healthy power and permission options are genuinely foreign to an addicted person.

The counselor instills protection immediately by creating a safe therapeutic climate. Safety and security are antecedent to self-actualization and precede any self-disclosure. You must render some security measures to prevent, as much as possible, any counterproductive interference from the outside, and do not prematurely open doors that the client is not prepared to enter.

As the counselor, you intensify your client's protection by never giving homework that has not been practiced in the counseling session first. You are responsible for knowing the client's home and/or treatment environment and how conducive it is to the proposed changes. To do otherwise would be sabotaging the counseling experience.

A counselor will seldom be quizzed about academic degrees, credentials, or competency (as important as they are) if he has consistently displayed power, potency, and protection with a client. Trust will evolve with your client as you provide these powerful principles and his confidence grows. Failing to do so will result in your client never returning to see you or, at best, "hanging in" while "hanging out."

VITAL THERAPEUTIC CONTRACTS

A therapeutic contract is a mutual agreement between the counselor and client, clarifying the intent and purpose of the counseling relationship.[15] Therapy contracts can be designed categorically. (These prototypes are either explicitly or implicitly included in this chapter.)

1. Exploratory Contract

Exploratory contracts define *what* and *how long* an issue will be probed. Your purpose is to give your client a choice and learn which direction he is willing to go. It helps overcome the notion that only the counselor knows what is happening. It adds the client's personal investment to the process.

The formulation of this contract considers your client's psychosocial history. The intent of this counseling agreement is to meet his decision to explore any presenting distresses and determine the direction of therapy.

This specific agreement offers you the opportunity to go "behind the scenes" and view the psycho-emotional drama that is frequently hidden. It prevents you from getting caught in a vacuum of trying to analyze and diagnose with surface data.

An example of an exploratory contract can be found in chapter 3 (see "Eliciting Highly Valued Criteria and Beliefs"). Before initiating it with your client, ask, "Are you willing to try on (check out, examine) the strength of your values and beliefs about what you are experiencing?" The word *willing* is an intentional one; *wanting, feeling like,* and *considering* are inadequate expressions, because they provide no grounds for a workable contract. Even if your client does not feel like or want to explore an issue, the real question is *whether* he will do so. Do not proceed until you both agree.

2. Change Contract

A change contract identifies specific behaviors or problems that your client seeks to resolve. Once you have explored a problem, the next step is to find out his commitment to change. In dealing with those who have addictive disorders, a change contract is the crux of the counseling relationship.

A chemically dependent person may try to manipulate you into concentrating on "exploration" rather than "transformation." The addict is tempted to believe that if he knows the "whys" of his drinking, using, overeating, or under-eating, the problem will be solved. I get irritated when

I witness counselors who accept this as a legitimate agenda. This type of agreement produces "why-ners" (the clients who whine over everything imaginable). This is called the "pity-pot syndrome."

Throughout the counseling period, you will be negotiating and renegotiating change contracts. These mini-treaties are the framework of a treatment plan. They help chart the course for counseling and measure the client's progress. I suggest that every session should begin with a review of the change contract.

The change contract is a "willful" decision, not a "needful" one. Anyone who needs to change has little motivation for life-long transformations. A person's will (not self-will) empowers him to act on what enhances self-growth and seriously assesses the cost. Change releases us from old alliances and confronts us with a new, unpredictable future.

Muriel James comments on the value of self-contracting:

"Breaking through to freedom is a lifelong task, never fully achieved. New goals emerge as though on the horizon, yet the process itself of moving toward the horizon of freedom is exciting and valuable. The process [contract for change] lends meaning to life and helps answer the questions, 'Who am I?' and 'What am I doing?'"[16]

3. Closure Contract

Although the magnitude of the first two therapy agreements is significant, I am convinced the closure contract is the most critical. This covenant deals with the psychoemotional "escape hatches" that your client could take to obstruct lasting change, and it closes these escape routes. No sincere behavior alteration will occur until a closure contract is in place.

The term *escape hatch* was popularized by transactional analysts. I was introduced to this concept in my clinical training forty years ago, and TA is still a viable model for counseling in the twenty-first century.[17]

My years of experience even after retirement taught me the lasting value and professional security in using these therapy contracts. I would never consider counseling the chemically dependent or anyone without these contracts, considering the history of self-defeating behavior.

The theory of escape hatches evolved from the formative work of Eric Berne, who developed the concepts of TA and, most significantly, life scripts. Dr. Harry Boyd, who was my TA mentor and one of my clinical supervisors, helped to refine escape hatches in relation to early child decisions regarding one's life script. This teaching is predicated on the belief that as children, we crystallize, or freeze, our experiences and decisions in warped time frames. Time is "now and forever" to a child. No matter how distorted or irrational a decision appears to the "Adult ego state," the inner child of the past accepts it as fact or reality.[18]

A child's early decisions are related to the psychological positions he takes regarding the worth of himself and others. Berne used these now-familiar postures: "I'm okay, you're not okay," "you're okay, I'm not okay," "I'm not okay, you're not okay," and "I'm okay, you're okay." Escape hatches are early functional decisions that the child can use whenever he must survive the distresses of his life.[19] The "trap doors" are described later.

An escape hatch is believed to be the way out because other options are closed. Exercising the escape hatches will reveal degrees of dysfunction from neuroses to severe pathologies.

Psychological or Physical Homicide

The operative theme of this issue is "I will get rid of those who get in my way (I'm okay, you're not)." This is acted out through verbal put-downs, emotional abuse, or a condescending attitude. Physically, it is manifested by physical abuse or eventual homicide. This person's primary behavior is intimidation.

Decisional Psychosis

Another option for abandoning a healthy decision is to "cop out" and enter a psychotic state. This thematic decision is "I'm crazy, you're crazy, and life's crazy—nothing and no one is okay." This behavior is deployed whenever a situation seems too difficult to handle (for some people, this happens frequently).

An individual portrays this neurotically when playing dumb and stupid or becomes so distraught that he enters the condition known as "depression." Depression in its foremost state can be depicted as being "hapless (no direction), helpless (no choices), hopeless (no promise), and humpless (no energy)." Going "crazy" and "being locked up" (psychologically) mean that the person does not have to be responsible for himself or others. The most common symptoms are mental confusion, fear of losing control, emotional constriction, and the inability to be decisive.

Psychological or Physical Suicide

The modal theme of this early decision is "I will get away from those individuals and events I can't manage (I'm not okay, you are)." The client is more at home in a "one-down" position, although he resents it. He chooses relationships and activities that reinforce his sense of inadequacy. He tends to let others make decisions for him and yet remains angry about feeling controlled. This is the most common theme in the life of the chemically dependent.

He may physically carry out this type of self-negation through physical scarring or suicide. It could be the final act of declaring, "I will punish you for not loving me enough to make up for the loss of loving myself."

Psychological and Emotional Health

One early decision that some children make is not an escape maneuver. It is the healthy resolution to "get on with my life no matter what happens." They acknowledge the worth of themselves and others by adopting the view "I'm okay, you're okay," and they are dedicated to personal and social fulfillment. This is never the position of the person addicted to chemicals. Until each escape hatch is nailed shut, the final option cannot be executed.

Each escape hatch commands your attention when counseling your client, and a closure contract is recommended before you arrange ongoing counseling. Insist that these contracts be made as your condition for being his counselor, despite the client's reluctance. Remember that the contracts are for his protection and yours.

A CLOSURE CONTRACT GUIDE

The following guide is suggested for closing escape hatches. Like all the exercises in this book, apply them to yourself before anyone else.

Have your client take a deep breath and exhale slowly. Ask him to describe the clothing he has on. This step is designed to get him into an adult ego state. This will be supported by clear thinking and "grown-up" words, free from significant emotional responses. Be sure that his posture is erect but not rigid and his legs or arms are uncrossed (if crossed, this could be like the childhood game of "king's X" meaning he does not have to tell the truth since his fingers or arms are crossed; this undermines the contract). A child believes in this myth.

Ask your client to repeat each statement below. It is all right if he thinks the exercise is phony or mechanical; it will still be effective. Get closure on the first statement before continuing. Use the words as they are written, because the statements are constructed to get the appropriate closure to each escape hatch.

1. "It's okay for me to feel like killing someone. I will not, accidentally or on purpose, no matter what happens."
2. "It's okay for me to feel like going crazy. I will not, accidentally or on purpose, no matter what happens."
3. "It's okay for me to feel like killing myself. I will not, accidentally or on purpose, no matter what happens."

Allow enough time for him to process each contract thoroughly. Be alert to words such as *but* or *sometimes* or failure to include the word *accidentally* in the contract. These common modifications suggest that his inner child is trying to negate the potency and truth of the pact. Pay close attention to the phrase "feel like." You are not giving *permission to act on* the feeling, only to "feel like" doing it. Affirming his feelings, without the need to act on them, offers great emotional release. You will normally hear a person sigh after this contract is made, which suggests relief.

REMEMBER TO DISSOCIATE THE THOUGHT OR FEELING FROM THE BEHAVIOR!

This procedure is useful in contracting for other issues such as anger without violence, crying without falling apart, feeling sexy without incest, rape, or promiscuity, and other problem behaviors. Installing these contracts with your client helps him to recognize that though feelings cannot be controlled, *behaviors* can be constructively channeled.

Let me emphasize that you avoid intensive or regressive counseling with anyone who has not satisfactorily completed a contract relative to each escape hatch. If your client is unwilling or hesitant to make one of these agreements without a specific duration, you can set a time frame. Mutually agree on the time of the contract (for example, "as long as you are in counseling" or "until I talk with you again").

I do not want to minimize the intensive dynamics of addiction counseling. You will be addressing major issues and behavioral problems. The appropriate time for focusing on family-of-origin concerns or mental disorders is when a strong abstinence/sobriety program has been established. You will discover my firm conviction regarding this principle in addiction counseling. I constantly had to remind my patients, "You drink and use not because you have problems. You have problems due to your drinking or using."

This is the reason for using potency, permission, and protection as all-inclusive tools when you install contracts. You and your client will be grateful for the effort spent in getting them firmly in place. You will know that you have been successful, to that point, by way of your client's willingness to continue.

CHAPTER 3

GROUNDING THE COUNSELING PROCESS

Alfred Adler, a physician and psychotherapist, was the creator of Adlerian psychology, sometimes called individual psychology. Adlerian psychology emphasizes the human need and ability to create positive social change and influence. Adler's teaching stressed the importance of nurturing feelings of belonging and striving for superiority. He held as core values equality, civil rights, mutual respect, and the advancement of democracy.

According to Adler, when a child feels encouraged, she senses being gifted and cherished and will mostly act in a cooperative way. When she gets dejected, she may act in harmful ways by conflicting, retreating, or resigning from activity. A positive self-concept is nurtured by encouragement, self-respect, and self-confidence. (You can explore this approach online by searching for "Adler School of Professional Psychology.")

Your chemically dependent client's self-concept is the antithesis of this idea. She will present herself as otherwise, but she feels defeated on the inside. Her addiction has manifested as destructive behaviors, psycho-emotional distress, and fractured relationships.

POSITIVE INTENTIONS

Where do you begin as her counselor? I discovered the power of NLP's "principle of positive intention." You may know this theory and heartily adopt the principle, but some have difficulty with it. This concept is built on the work of renowned family therapist, Virginia Satir. She adopted Adler's theory of child development and added it to her belief in positive affirmations. Her therapeutic process made a distinction between what a person said and what was *intended*. Richard Bandler, the codeveloper of NLP (with John Grinder), observed Satir's use of positive affirmation and was struck by the power and dynamics of her communication.[20]

Positive intention is one of the foundational theories of NLP. This is a philosophical position that behind each human behavior is a positive intention. Few of us, if any, act without some internal logic or strong belief. Adler was an ardent proponent of this theory. Despite how you experience someone else's actions, she is behaving sensibly (from her world view).

The behavior a person displays may appear disturbing or even pathological (such as drinking or using to excess). Until you can understand the values and beliefs that provide the backdrop for the behavior, you cannot adequately comprehend what is happening. You may attempt to criticize, analyze, or diagnose the situation and yet be far off in your evaluation.

One day, I was talking with a psychiatric nurse who was having a problem with the mother of a teenage girl. The nurse was involved in admitting the young girl to our adolescent unit. During the intake interview, she discovered that the girl had been arrested for prostitution and drug possession. While the nurse considered this typical behavior for someone addicted, her disturbance surfaced when she discovered that the girl's mother was responsible for the girl's prostitution.

The caring RN could not believe that any mother would stoop to this level. "If the mother loved her daughter," the nurse bellowed, "she would want to get her out of this environment! The mother is sicker than her daughter!" What the nurse did not know was how the mother perceived her own behavior. The nurse didn't inquire about the values and beliefs of the mother, who also had a history of prostitution. The nurse prejudged and sentenced the mother as unfit without exploring the mother's positive intent.

During the in-depth assessment, one of our counselors unveiled that the mother had been a prostitute since she was fourteen. She had been severely beaten and sexually assaulted as a child. She ran away from home to escape the trauma and developed a relationship with a professional pimp. The mother continued to be physically and sexually abused. She eventually broke away from this situation and learned to survive on the streets by herself. A few years later, she became pregnant from a "john." She wanted to have the baby and be a loving parent regardless of her childhood trauma. She was determined to be a good mother and to teach her child "how to survive." This novice mother lived in a world that was foreign to the nurse, and her behavior appeared reprehensible until others understood her logic and positive intent. She did the best she could with what she knew.

Affirming a person's positive intent is not condoning or accepting an unhealthy behavior. It is validating the person's *motivation* to do what is best or appropriate without approving the action. It is acknowledging her worthiness while avoiding judgment of the behavior. The actual behavior is the therapeutic issue that is addressed in the counseling process after the motivation is identified.

The idea of positive intent may be an obstacle to your clients, and some counselors won't accept the concept. They doubt that behaviors (especially addictive ones) have any underlying value. The clients may be wrought with guilt and shame, so it seems normal to deny that their actions could have positive motives. As a counselor, your challenge is to teach your clients the difference between behavior and intent. This is a crucial step in opening the client to the possibility of change. It is surprising and validating for a client when she uncovers this truth.

I hope you are persuaded of the importance of separating the function (or intent) of a behavior from the actual behavior. A person is more likely to alter a behavior when she understands the purpose and value of it, but you will not discover her intent or value by asking "why" questions. It is more effective to ask these questions: "*What* is it about this behavior that concerns you?" or "What is important to you about this behavior?" A "what" question gets to the underlying functions, intentions, values, and beliefs of the behavior.

The nurse who had difficulty understanding her patient's mother could have been a positive force in the treatment process had she exercised such skill. She could have had a deeper appreciation for the teenager's struggle with her mother and the fundamental issues involved in the addictive relationship. She later admitted her failure and learned from this experience. The mother was cooperative and fully engaged in the treatment of her daughter.

SIGNIFICANCE OF BELIEFS AND VALUES

A belief is the conviction that something is right or true.[21] A belief system includes frames of reference related to how you give order and meaning to your existence. How you behave, feel, and think evolves from your belief system. You form beliefs throughout life, beginning in infancy. Some beliefs are positive, and others are more negative. However, your belief system serves the following purposes.

Providing a Cognitive and Ethical Guide

Moral and ethical structures are woven from the fabric of early childhood teachings and experiences. If you did not have these structures, your ability to mature into adulthood would be impaired. As a child, you were taught to believe things that are not relevant to adulthood, yet you came to accept this belief system of "truth" and "reality" as the framework for your moral, ethical, and rational decisions. A child has limited abilities to adequately interpret or understand teachings, so it is not surprising if her belief systems are filled with distortions and omissions. This is why it is important to reassess the relevance of thoughts and beliefs in adulthood.

Constructing an Image of an Orderly World

For children (and adults), psycho-emotional stability depends on order and predictability in a world of chaos and turmoil. Abraham Maslow maintained that two basic requirements in the hierarchy of human needs are safety and security. His well-known thesis stressed that primary needs precede any drive toward self-actualization. You have an innate need to be safe and secure, and your ability to meet these needs helps to create self-confidence or the lack of it.

Forming Bonds with Others

Beliefs shape your self-concept and interpersonal relationships. How you see yourself and others is integral to the healthy or unhealthy relationships you establish. Your mastery of intimacy (effective bonding and detaching) is linked to what you believe about love, friendship, marriage, parenting, etc. Personal beliefs and perceptions are often the sources of fears regarding love and intimacy.

Counteracting Ontic Anxiety

The phrase *ontic anxiety* is attributed to the late existential theologian Paul Tillich. This kind of anxiety is distinct from psychic anxiety. Fritz Perls, considered by many to be the father of Gestalt therapy, referred to psychological anxiety as "stage fright." It has also been called "performance fear." (I am not including anxiety disorders that are evidenced by biochemical imbalances sometimes linked with mental illness.)

Ontic anxiety is the "fear of becoming authentic" or the "phobia of living life to the fullest." Those affected by this kind of anxiety ask, "Is there life after birth?" This is a daily question for those seeking sobriety.

A *value* determines how desirable or important it is to be or act in a particular way. Values, like beliefs, are learned. Your values define your ethical and moral boundaries. Values are a subset of a belief system, and beliefs are given levels of importance by your values. Thus, values and beliefs form a hierarchical system of behaviors that determine how you relate to others and experience reality.

Weighing What is Most or Least Important

What are your criteria for determining if something or someone is valuable? They include the time and energy you invest. You can tell someone that your family is important to you, but where in your daily or weekly schedule is your family given priority? Add up the hours that you apply to this value. There are periods when you choose one activity or relationship over another though they hold equal importance. Over time, the real priorities capturing your self-investment are the true values you honor. This is why values need to be weighed periodically and their significance audited.

Validating Self-Concept and Social-Image

Beliefs mold self-concept, and values validate self-concept and social image. We seldom live in isolation. We are created to be in community, and thus we are shaped by our relationships.

What you do verifies what is authentic or superficial about your values and beliefs. Values and beliefs that complement each other are validated with congruent behaviors.

Establishing Social Consciousness and Associations

Human beings are created for relationships. Each of us is a citizen of the global community, and values and beliefs operate in every social system from a family to a business conglomerate or international government. Community values are part and parcel of the laws, policies, and regulatory procedures used to maintain a social system. Our values either complement or conflict with this social consciousness, and this is a major struggle for most of us. (I assure you that it is for the individual trapped in addiction.)

Organizing Relevant Limits and Boundaries

Boundaries define the parameters of a relationship. Relationship boundaries formalize how two people interact and sustain their well-being. As a counselor, firmly fashion the boundaries of your professional relationship with every client from the moment you meet.

Family systems ruled by the addictive process experience convoluted boundaries. Twisted values and beliefs are active in this dysfunctional system, yet they hold the family together. No matter how misshapen the values appear, these are the "gems," or core dynamics, that offer hope for the potential change in your client and her family.

You will find a step-by-step exercise for your client in "Eliciting Highly Valued Criteria and Beliefs." You may want to use this exercise to explore your values and beliefs before experimenting with others.

Personal Values and Beliefs Inventory

Take a few minutes to complete the following inventory of your personal values and beliefs. Clarify them as a way of enhancing your skills.

1. List three of your primary values, and write them down in order of importance.

2. Are any of these values relevant to what you do in counseling a person? In what way do your values apply?

3. Identify three of your significant beliefs, and write them down in order of importance.

4. Choose one or more of the beliefs and values you listed, and write a personal credo regarding the responsibilities of a professional counselor.

5. In what way could your values and beliefs block effective counseling?

6. In what way could your values and beliefs expand your effectiveness in counseling?

ELICITING HIGHLY VALUED CRITERIA AND BELIEFS

The following exercise guides your client through identifying values and beliefs. It helps her recognize how they affect life events and experiences. This opens the door for you to explore the hidden, secret places within her. This guide merges the theories of TAs and NLP, and I assure you that it will be extremely valuable in your practice.

Have your client get into a relaxed state. It is important that she be in a "Child ego state" (unlike the work you do when closing escape hatches). Closure contracts require the person to be in the adult ego state. Ask factual questions ("What time of day is it?" "Describe what you're wearing," "Name three people in this group," etc.). Note: These are not "feelings" or "attitudes" just "facts."

When eliciting her values and beliefs, it is useful for the feelings to surface. The more you keep her focused on problems related to her history of chemical dependence, the better. The following narrative helps to accomplish this objective. Get comfortable, and use your own words when directing the process.

1. "Recall an experience in which you reacted with strong or intense emotions. The experience can be a positive or negative one." (Ask for only one experience; precise recall is not necessary.)

2. "Tell me about the experience. What do you see, hear, feel, etc." Embellish what she shares by asking her to see

colors, sense textures (rough, smooth, etc.), feel the temperature (warm, cold, etc.), and listen to noises (voice tones, etc.)

3. "What is it about this experience that seems to cause your strong reaction?" You will hear her state personal values and beliefs. Pay attention to the experience and behaviors, not the feelings. Any value or belief results in related behaviors and feelings give intensity to the event, especially if connected to her CD.)

4. Restate the value or belief as you heard it. "So what is important to you is (to be a good parent, to be loyal, to be a loving friend, to be responsible, etc.)." You will get a positive or negative response. If it is negative, have your client restate it, followed by your restatement, or you can return to step three. Do not move to step five until you have agreement.

5. If the value or belief is vague, ask for a defined meaning. "What does it mean for you to be (a good parent, etc.)?" These descriptive words will clarify the *belief* and even move to a higher one. The same is true regarding a value.

6. State the belief as you heard it, and get a firm yes that this is what she means. Ask her, "Did you meet or violate your (value or belief) in this situation? If so, in what way?"

7. Ask her, "Is this value or belief still important or useful to you today? In what way is it or is it not?"

8. Ask her, "In what way has this value (belief) affected your relationship with (a significant other)?" If she is unsure or denies any affect, ask if she is willing to check out her perception. This is a way of breaking through denial.

This process is only for eliciting and clarifying a client's values and beliefs. You are seeking to discover the appropriateness of behaviors in relation to her beliefs and values. You are not to change her beliefs or ask if she wants to alter the belief or value; that will come later. You are uncovering her positive intent.

CHAPTER 4

COUNSELING IN ACTION

Your ability to retain your client in treatment is equal to the leverage (psychosocial force or power used to influence change) available to you. Leverage has internal and external factors, and it is what has motivated your client to agree to counseling in the first place. It relates to the "bottom line" set by his family, boss, or a judge. Our hospital program had many referrals from judges who mandated treatment as a condition for deferred sentencing. This was powerful leverage, to say the least.[22]

USING LEVERAGE IN ADDICTION COUNSELING

Your clients will experience at least three stages during counseling or treatment. They will not enter a stage without having gone through the preceding one. The movement through these stages is prompted by using leverage.

All counseling, but especially addiction counseling, begins with the initial factor of leverage. Treatment will not advance without leverage to influence your client's decisions. The incentive for change is within him no matter the source of the leverage. Any leverage is potentially useful if your client connects a personal value to it; if there is no value associated, he has little motivation to respond, much less change.

Experience in this field tells me that few if any clients show up wanting help without some kind of outside influence, even if they say otherwise. Someone or something has led him to this moment of truth, and he needs professional assistance. At this point, he does not believe he's chemically dependent, an alcoholic, a drug addict, or sick. All he feels is that the distress in his life needs to end. Normally, this stress is the leverage you need to explore.

Let us look at some verbal clues to how his decision for help is realized with the applied leverage. These are sample reactions, and other comments by your client which could fit into one of the stages.

STAGE ONE: EXTERNALIZING LEVERAGE

The addicted person enters treatment or counseling because of real or suspected pressure. This could be anything from a court order to the potential loss of a job or marriage. You can easily identify the external leverage when he makes comments like, "I *cannot* drink or use because (I will go to jail, my spouse will leave me, I will lose my job, etc.)." Typically someone has set a "bottom-line" and initially this becomes leverage.

Use the external leverage, which normally has a bottom line, to your and the client's advantage. The external forces are most likely to override your client's strong denial. That is why it is called external leverage. The addict feels he's being "forced" to obtain help or something serious will happen. He doesn't believe that he has a problem with drinking or using and says, "I wouldn't drink so much if *they* would get off my case!"

Do not be tempted to say, "Unless you *want* to get help, treatment will do you no good!" Know what the bottom-line is from each interacting system impacting the addict's choice for getting help. You will use these often during stage one.

Be sure to couple your client's positive intent with his external leverage and need for treatment. The addict's beliefs and values need to be consistently grounded in every step and stage. The strength of the bottom line is no stronger than your client's associated beliefs and values.

STAGE TWO: INTERNALIZING LEVERAGE

Sometimes your client can progress to this stage rapidly. It will depend on the acuteness of the detox or other impairments. Others make slower progress and have greater problems internalizing what they learn.

The focus will be on your client's admission of the deleterious consequences of his addiction. He may not fully embrace the notion that he is an addict (this is some of the carry-over from stage one), but he is a willing to see the correlation between his drinking or using and the effects on others.

Stage two will reveal his gradual movement from admission to acceptance. His words will disclose an attitude shift when he admits that the drug habit "probably" has some effect on others. This shift is a significant one. You will hear him make comments like "I *will not* drink or use because (I am hurting my family, I am tired of fighting the guilt and shame, my work or school is being affected, etc.)."

This is when the chemically dependent may experience fantasies and dreams about drinking or using. Help him to not resist or fear these experiences. Let him see and understand them as unconscious activities or options for dealing with compulsions, cravings, and feelings.

The addict's loss of chemicals will mean doing later grief counseling related to his void. During this stage, he needs to address the loss or impairment of relationships and associations that have revolved around his drinking or using.

Help your client develop an "anti-sabotage plan" and "future pace" (or practice) options for dealing with sobriety and possible relapse. Have him list ways that he could undermine his progress made to date. Role-play situations he might encounter in the "real" world and new behavioral alternatives for maintaining abstinence/sobriety. Keep the issue of *protection* in mind.

You can begin a moderate shift from directive counseling to insight therapy (and blending both) as you work through this stage. This is because your client is able to accept ownership for the outcomes of his drinking or using. There is less need for external leverage. More reflective counseling methods will see increasing gains. No decision the addict has made to this point is more serious than the ultimate acceptance and surrender to the addiction. The leverage is now internalized.

STAGE THREE: ACTUALIZING LEVERAGE

The final stage witnesses the integration of the client's insights into all areas of his life. He prompts his changes rather than waiting to be confronted by the counselor or peers. You hear him say, "I *choose* not to drink or use because (I can be close to and enjoy my family, I find pleasure and joy in other ways, I am grateful for the opportunity to live my life fully, etc.)."

Your client can apply healthy, adaptive behaviors and problem-solving skills to internal and external conflicts. He will need to return to each preceding stage as he moves from abstinence to recovery.

There is always a circular dimension to counseling. Each new issue or problem in a person's life will be processed through all stages. You will guide him through the natural increments of each stage and may repeat them when essential.

You will need to remind your client that change is a dynamic, not a static, adventure. No person should expect to get all his problems solved through counseling. Unfortunately, this could take years, and for some psychotherapists, this is the norm. You are working with an addiction, and this is a present-day issue not requiring long-term, regressive therapy. The skills acquired through counseling give your client the ability to resolve other concerns beyond the addiction. Support groups are helpful, but intensive counseling is not needed to address all his CD problems. There are certain preexisting complications that require additional psycho-emotional treatment once the person has completed CD treatment. Some CD professionals recommend at least two years of sobriety before initiating psychotherapy. I don't hold hard and fast to this timeline, but my experience confirms a need for a reasonable period before psychotherapy happens when sobriety is well established.

When new concerns emerge, it is appropriate to interface teachings from earlier stages to any presenting problem. To understand this fully, I break down the goals of counseling.

COUNSELING GOALS WITH THE CHEMICALLY DEPENDENT

Your skills and gifts as a counselor have minimal value if you do not know where you're going with a client. It is like being dressed up for a dance, but no one told you where the dance is or how to get there. Counseling goals assist you in guiding your clients toward their desired outcomes. It is true that each person is unique and that counseling is to be individualized, but you cannot overlook the primary goals that are essential to an addict's recovery.[23]

Three goals correspond to the three stages of leverage presented earlier. They could be called levels of therapeutic growth or even stages of progress. The classification is not important. Your ability to escort your client on this journey is central.

These goals and objectives are successive, like those of leveraging a client. Each step usually overlaps and builds on the previous one, but you need to move through the levels sequentially. Do not push your client too quickly through this process. Be sensitive to his readiness to go toward the goals.

A goal is a long-term and overarching outcome, and an objective is a concrete and measurable activity or behavioral change. I am aware that not everyone agrees with these distinctions. For the moment, allow yourself to accept this concept, even if you have a different opinion. The following three general goals are attained by meeting five objectives. The objectives are specific and, when concluded, should achieve each desired goal.

GOAL ONE: ABSTINENCE

Abstinence is refraining from the use of any addictive, mind- or mood-altering chemical. Your client will need to be led, not forced, through each objective. The use of non-directive counseling will facilitate this stage. Dr. Carl Rogers, the founder of humanistic psychology and client-centered therapy, was a proponent of this model, even though he later stopped using this term or claiming they were synonymous.[24]

Distress

The absence of a drug can result in psychological or physical withdrawal or both. The experience of not being "high" or "stoned" requires your client to undergo distress. Many professionals adopt the dictum, "Without distress, one is infrequently challenged to change." The chemically dependent person is habituated to drinking and using to avoid the distress. A contract not to drink or use is compulsory before serious counseling is initiated. (Use the closure contract.)

Do not attempt to comfort your client at the expense of his distress. Give support, but direct (not force) him toward his pain. Talk therapy, centering on feelings, or role-playing actual, intoxicating events will increase the "dis-ease" for him. This is the means to help him look for alternatives to drinking or using to deal with distress.

Identification

Your client can start to see that he has something in common when he hears of the trials and tribulations of others in a group. To identify with another person opens the door to the new reality of not being alone. This is the prelude to self-recognition. Asking the client if he identifies with another group member is a more subtle approach to reliving his addiction.

Recognition

Self-discovery is threatening. Sometimes your client remains in ignorance, not due to mental limitations but because what remains hidden alters his reality. Change and growth require self-knowing. Out of recognition comes the seedling of a new self-image. Recognizing himself in others is the start of self-acceptance.

Admission

Your client succumbs to the knowledge that he is an addict. He begins to state, "I am an alcoholic/drug addict." This is the letting go dimension that precedes acceptance of, or surrender to, the actual disease. Until he has made this public acknowledgment to his peers, there is no progress. Though the words are experienced as cursory, the ritual of the group helps your client start to make a mental and emotional connection. The counseling will focus on helping the client associate the consequences of his drinking or using to the direct choices he has made. He did not choose to become addicted, but he is responsible for the outcomes of it.

Compliance

Compliance is the ability to "go with the flow" and cease resisting the contract for remaining abstinent. It means giving in without giving up. You will witness your client responding to your directives with little or no questioning. This is one way for him to admit that he needs help and is powerless over his affairs. Naive counselors are prone to believe that this is a sign of acceptance. It is compliance, and it is a major step for your client during the first stage.

Giving assignments for attending 12 Step meetings or reading from the Big Book of Alcoholics Anonymous are effective in assessing the client's degree of compliance. However, do not overwork him and set him up for failure. Keep everything within reason. If your client has reading difficulties or is illiterate, have him find someone who can help with a reading assignment. Create the possibilities for success.

GOAL TWO: SOBRIETY

Sobriety is learning to alter one's lifestyle without the need or desire for mood-altering chemicals. This does not minimize the times when urges surface. There may be circumstances when a physician must monitor your client with nonaddictive, psychotropic drugs. If your client has a history of clinical depression or bipolar disorder, for example, sobriety includes responsible use and close supervision of his medications.

Failure to keep this issue central to sobriety is another form of drug abuse. Your client will venture through this level.

Acceptance

A liberating truth brings a freedom to receive the gifts of sobriety. Your client may know and believe that his disease is not the essence of who he is but the absence of what he can be. Declaring himself an "alcoholic/drug addict" is not accepting a label; it is proclaiming freedom from the bondage of addiction.

There will be congruence in his words, feelings, attitude, and behavior. This will be even clearer when you begin practicing the reframing and future pacing methods presented in the next chapter.

Surrender

The transformation from abstinence to sobriety is most evident when your client yields to a higher power than himself. He celebrates the release of control and engages the power of living on a natural high.

Acceptance and *surrender* are not synonymous. Acceptance is a decision of receiving one's addiction as a human condition. Surrender is a transpersonal act of accepting responsibility for one's life and not playing the victim. Steps one to three of AA and NA are internalized.

Conversion

This is not religious "conversion" but the transformation of his beliefs, values, and behaviors. Your client's words and actions are consistently complementary. There is an integration of beliefs, values, and behaviors resulting in regard for himself and others. Steps four and five of AA and NA can be initiated. Assimilate this information into the counseling sessions.

Action

Your client now acts on what he says. He is genuinely "walking the walk" and "talking the talk." He follows through with his verbal commitments. He follows through with new learning and is honest when the struggle gets difficult. He knows when to ask for help and accepts confrontation and feedback willingly.

Adjustment

Your client is braving a new world without a distorted reality. Do not mistake this as *readjusting*—this is unlike anything he has known before. Like a newborn, the sphere of sobriety is a mystery. Learning new coping skills is vital to addressing normal distresses as they arise in his daily routine.

GOAL THREE: RECOVERY

Recovery is reclaiming the gift of one's life as a special and common human being. Your client is not special because of who he is but due to his inherent worthiness as a person. He is common because he has discovered that he participates in a community of mutually caring people. He has learned to live in common unity with others. He has a homecoming with family (sometimes) and friends when he celebrates this common bond. He is delivered from his egocentric past to enjoy the beauty of who he is in fellowship with significant others.

This final level for your client will provide the following:

Readjustment

He will succeed and fail in making the right decisions or responding in appropriate ways, and these become ongoing challenges. Living is a matter of learning to adjust and readjust to the complexities and difficulties of his life. This is how one copes with the stresses and distresses of daily events.

Resolution

He will be learning and relearning constructive behaviors for resolving conflict, forgoing perfection, and admitting mistakes. Asking for help is seen as strength. He resolves to act rather than react to confrontation and other actions by those he encounters.

Reconciliation

He is bridging the gap of shattered relationships and restoring the foundations of meaningful activities. He is offering and receiving forgiveness. He releases his hold on the past and the past's hold on him. In the spiritual realm this is conversion, confession, acceptance and giver of forgiveness.

Restitution

He makes amends even though it may not be possible in every case (a person is deceased or is unwilling to listen). Restitution could be a financial or physical act. His authentic restitution is living fully in recovery and sharing his story with others. He does not take sobriety or life for granted and lives every day in gratitude.

Re-creation

He is rebirthed. A new consciousness is unearthed. He dances and sings to the rhythms of life. He shouts a new credo in the wind, "Life is good! I am good! You are good!" He has unwrapped some of his gifts of recovery; there are many such as healing, hope, serenity, forgiveness, love, compassion, service, and more!

The road to recovery is never ending. There is no final destination. It wanders through living history and is the legacy of every new generation. The client who successfully travels this road embraces an inheritance as a benefactor, not as a creator.

CHAPTER 5

TREATMENT GOALS WITH CHEMICALLY DEPENDENT ADOLESCENTS

The stages and goals of addition counseling are similar for adults and adolescents. However, you need to include specific factors when counseling an adolescent client. Don't forget that the psycho-emotional development of a teenager is notably impeded by alcohol and/or drug use. You will not be dealing with a typical adolescent (the same can be said of adults whose development was impeded at the onset of their addiction). The developmental issues are still prominent in treatment. The older teens will think and act in more immature ways, and the younger ones will appear even more childish in their behaviors and attitudes. Judith Marks Mishne correctly stated the obvious:

"The easy availability and use of drugs which cause regression have made it difficult for some adolescents to develop and sustain

meaningful emotional involvements with others and to tolerate frustration in the move toward mature adulthood. Adolescents to-day commonly depend on external factors such as music, peers, and drugs for psychological stimulation. They have little experience in tolerating ambivalence, ambiguity, grief, and mourning."[25]

As a backdrop, I give a generalized review of the phases of adolescent development in contrast to youth with addiction problems. This will be an oversimplification, but you can note the development of chemically dependent adolescents in relation to normal adolescent growth. In the hospital we had adolescents in treatment as young as twelve years old with the onset of drug use at age nine. They were not experimenting or "acting out" it was their way of surviving in a critically dysfunctional family.

ADOLESCENT DEVELOPMENTAL PHASES

Early Adolescence (12–13 Years)

During this early period, the adolescent begins to shift from primary parental values and beliefs to a tempered state of separation. She displays an exaggerated independence and acts this out through rebellious attitudes and behaviors toward most adults, especially her parents.

The most blatant way to manifest this independence is through radical conformity to peer group values (hairstyles, trendy clothes, "groupie" activities, etc.). These new attachments are an effort to avoid feelings of loneliness and isolation.

This is a time of erratic mood swings. The teen undergoes bodily changes, which creates a sense of disharmony, resulting in self-consciousness, shame, and inner and interpersonal unrest. She is struggling with her body image through an integration of self-perception and that of peers.

If she is caught in the cycle of drug addiction, her behavior will display more severe reactions during this phase. Her normal struggles are compounded because her drug use has its own set of obstacles.

Drugs, including alcohol, distort the self-image, trigger guilt and shame, alienate one from healthy support systems, and alter attitudes and behaviors. The biochemical reactions of ingested chemicals baffle the brain's response to normal psychophysical growth. The emotions become blunted, the mind is progressively stunted, and the body cannot adequately produce the hormones or cellular structures for physical maturation.

In essence, the adolescent is stuck in time and will not progress until the drug use stops. The important skill of value development is thwarted. She is unable to make value decisions because of the distortions, deceptions, and misconceptions masked in her CD.

There will be exaggerated mood swings, acute rebellion, radical (deluded) self-sufficiency, and an obsessive preoccupation with appearance (not neatness) during her active using or drinking.

The young adolescent does not function at an abstract level of thinking. She is a pragmatist and needs everything to be concrete. If it cannot be touched, seen, heard, felt, or smelled, it does not matter. If you are counseling this teen, do not overlook this reality, or you will have major communication problems.

Middle Adolescence (14–17 Years)

This phase is characterized by an even more intense emotional life and movement toward closer heterosexual relationships (sometimes homosexual), which may result in a significant "first love." There is a corresponding increase in detaching from parents. Peers are consistently more influential than parents or other adults. Being seen with parents can be embarrassing for these supersensitive youth.

As the adolescent withdraws from her parents, you witness a correlating escalation of moodiness, puffed-up ego, self-absorption, and amplified sensitivity to the body. The reverberations of this sensitivity are exhibited by increased sexual arousal and anxiety over how to act sexually. Drug abuse is often associated with the beginning of sexual activity at this age.

Often the adolescent discovers that drinking or using is an effective tension reliever. She overcomes the sense of guilt when violating primary values related to self-identity. Instead of the typical distancing from parents and family, which any adolescent needs for individuating, the chemically dependent teenager lives in estrangement. She believes that parents, adults, and institutions are the sources of suffocation and negation of her life. Little does she realize how addiction has driven a wedge between her and her external world. The only closeness she knows is a pseudo-intimacy with peers who also use. In contrast to the early adolescent, the "middler" has more cognitive abilities, though they are impaired by her addiction.

This teen is more realistic, objective, and analytical. She needs a balance between abstract or theoretical reflection and concreteness. She resents being taken literally but simultaneously tends to perceive what others say and do in literal terms.

The chemically dependent adolescent, however, has difficulty employing critical thinking. Thought patterns and memory retention are besieged due to the drugs.

The middle adolescent's interests, skills, and talents have dawned, and self-esteem is more stable. She is ordinarily more certain about what beliefs and values are important to her, even those parental values and beliefs that are unacceptable.

It is common for the drug-addicted youth to operate out of a primitive value system known as *narcing*. Narcing is considered "copping out" on a fellow drug user (other slang terms are *coke head, junkie, tweaker,* etc.). She will rarely risk transgressing this law of survival.

For a counselor, it is hard to understand the paranoia that surfaces when asking a teenager to self-disclose. Though middle-age addicted adolescents have minimal or convoluted values, they hold fast to the rule, "Don't talk."

Late Adolescence (18–19 Years)

The last phase is one of consolidation and stabilization of personality. There is more clarity and purposeful actions, constancy of emotions, stable self-esteem, and more mature functioning.

Narcissism is diminished, and there is a greater tolerance for negotiation, compromise, and delayed gratification. The older adolescent searches and longs for support from others in developing a social conscience.

There is an increased capacity for abstract reflecting, critical thinking, and gaining insight. The adolescent is capable of looking somewhat objectively at herself and others. Adult and parent relationships are more significant.

In the life of the chemically dependent teen, conflicts continually escalate proportionate to the increase in drinking or using. The repetition of self-medication hastens the pathological development. She has a low tolerance for frustration, little social skills for resolving conflicts, and a pandemic, depressed affect.[26]

Counseling Goals with Adolescents

Social functioning is basic to the adolescent's drive toward self-acceptance. Therefore, the first goal of counseling will be examining how drinking or using activities interfere with social functioning or attaining personal goals.

The concepts and practical skills in this book direct the adolescent toward confronting these realities. The approaches keep her in the here and now. There is no subtle or hidden agenda to analyze the reasons for drinking or using. The nucleus of your counseling is to connect the results of drinking to her desired outcomes.

The second goal is to help the adolescent develop skills to handle social and peer pressure without resorting to drinking or using. Abstinence contracts during the period of counseling are without exception. (This contract will not work with teens being treated at an outpatient site. Aftercare is a different matter. An in-patient facility has the structure and staff to monitor the activities of adolescents.) If this is not possible, have frequent group sessions with peers so that oversight is somewhat feasible. Set your bottom line regarding drug use during treatment. This should be included in the written abstinence contract and signed by your client and her parents/guardians.

The third counseling goal is to provide peer support for your client in coping with the feelings of being different, an outsider, straight, etc. The 12 Step programs are the most beneficial resources for creating alternative support groups during the ongoing stress of counseling. Therapy complements (AA, NA, and corresponding 12 Step programs) bring balance to counseling. In your treatment plan, establish the requirements for participating in adolescent 12 Step meetings when not attending a counseling group.

I discourage individual therapy with chemically dependent persons whether they are adults or adolescents. I agree that there are times when there is no other option (incest issues, sexual abuse, disclosing criminal activity, etc.). You may determine later the importance of your client disclosing this in the group. Group therapy is the only therapeutic setting I have seen to be long-term effective with teenagers and adults. The power and peer pressure of group dynamics are most influential with adolescents. They are also adept at confronting the inconsistencies of their peers when they understand the dangers of keeping secrets and narcing.

Help the addicted teen to develop healthy values and beliefs instead of clarifying them. Again, value clarification with chemically dependent teens is ineffective, because value development happens during this time of growth, and their drug addiction blocks it. Lectures and group instruction on values are critical once your teen is practicing abstinence on a regular basis. Usually an addicted youth has limited clarity and few conceived values due to her inhibited growth. Educating her about rules, values, and beliefs is a dominant counseling objective.

While sobriety is one overarching goal of treatment, the average youth lacks an image of what this means. You need to help her develop abstinence/sobriety models that are consistent with her emerging beliefs and values. This is a tremendous quest for you and her. Images emerge from the constant tussles of shattering old illusions and discovering new behaviors, meanings, and perspectives. Images are sharpened by practicing these fresh teachings and replacing the seasoned behaviors of addiction. In conjunction with the previous objective, you want to facilitate the restructuring (reframing) of the adolescent's self-image and self-independence.

She needs to experience the balance of autonomy and accountability and of self-confidence and humility. She is building a future while living in the moment.

Provide structured tasks to help the adolescent manage extreme mood swings, depressive periods, and interpersonal conflict. Discover what talents she has (music, art, writing, etc.), and create therapeutic interventions actively using her interests and talents.

Throughout the counseling sessions, a foundational goal is to create a surrogate family system in which the teenager can express her feelings openly and appropriately. She can learn problem-solving skills for daily living.

THE NEED FOR FAMILY AND OTHERS IN TREATMENT

While this book concentrates on counseling the chemically dependent rather than family counseling, I am convinced of the necessity of including family or significant others in treatment. Family counseling is critical for those with a chemically dependent member. Our hospital admission policy for the CDU required family participation or involvement of significant others. CD is a systemic disease. One does not become addicted in isolation, and without question, treatment and recovery are ineffective without interfacing support structures.[27]

You should assess the appropriateness and capability of each family member who is part of the treatment early on. Some families have high levels of toxicity and histories of physical and emotional abuse. When I was responsible for family education and counseling, I spent time with the family to determine the degree of interaction and communication I could expect. I learned about significant others who might get involved. An employer, teacher, pastor, friend, or any person who had a vested interest was a wonderful asset in treatment.

For the first two weeks of inpatient treatment, the loved one has no contact (phone calls or visits). Today's digital explosion means no use of iPhones, iPods, or computers, so there is some "social detox" for every member of the family. Families and significant others make treatment commitments to attend education sessions and support groups in preparation for "Family Week."

Almost everything in a chemically dependent person's life centers on her drug of choice. Her conduct in the family, at work, or at school is normally reactionary. Her ability to act responsibly and dependably is unpredictable. She is manipulative and will make many promises to change. Any effort on the part of a family member or parent to help only exacerbates the problem. The central organizing principle for this family dynamic is the behavior and drinking or drug use of the addict. Sometimes professionals have labeled this an "alcoholic family system," which I argue is not appropriate. The family is enmeshed in the chemically dependent person's control of the family system and participates in the dysfunction of the addict, but this does not mean that the family is addicted, chemically dependent, or alcoholic.

The family mirrors the dysfunction of the addict/alcoholic. In order to understand how this happens, I want to examine child development in general. One of the developmental tasks of the family is to mirror a child's personal identity. A child comes to know who she is by getting feedback from others. Every healthy family has some dysfunction, but a healthy system can quickly identify and admit to failure. The unhealthy family is oblivious to this dynamic. It accepts the dysfunction as normal, because other families act the same way in their eyes.

The family caught in the throes of a member being chemically dependent is so chaotic that it mirrors its dysfunction to the child and one another. Neurotic and pathological behaviors can be mutually satisfying as long as those involved believe these behaviors provide the family members with what they want or need.

Coping and defense strategies are learned in relation to the normal stresses through which any family journeys. However, the child of an addicted parent develops chronic reactive behaviors to deal with the protracted storms of family life (versus the periodic storms in a normal family). It is common for a teacher to request a conference with the parents because their child is acting out at school. She gets into fights with peers or withdraws and does not participate in activities. Children of chemically dependent adults have distorted self-images and are unable to separate their personal feelings from others. This sorting of feelings is an important aspect of counseling during the treatment process, and it becomes more evident when family members are asked to share their feelings during Family Week. Each member needs education about the disease's all-encompassing threat to health and well-being.

The family as a whole develops defense mechanisms in an effort to survive the turbulence. Two primary defenses include rationalizing and minimizing, which the chemically dependent practice well. Bill Wilson, the cofounder of AA, wrote in a letter:

> *"You know what our genius for rationalization is. If, to ourselves, we fully justify one slip, then our rationalizing propensities are almost sure to justify another one, perhaps with a different set of excuses. But one justification leads to another and presently we are back on the bottle full time."*[28]

Family members get accomplished at rationalizing the behavior of the addict. The mother tells her children, "Your father's had a bad day, and he needs time to relax, so give him space." Interactions are overwhelmed by fear and anxiety, because family members never know what the addict will say or do when drinking or using.

Minimizing is a major challenge to a family that habitually believes that everything will be okay if it can just fix the loved one. Family members say, "She's the one who needs help, not me!" They are ignorant and in denial regarding the acuteness of the problem.

The chemically addicted adolescent must have family support and active participation in her treatment. Failure to include the family (or a surrogate/foster family) in ongoing therapy only leads to relapse. Her sobriety is endangered when the family refuses to see that her enabling behavior contributes to the chaotic environment. Health is impossible when you must live, or really exist, in an unhealthy atmosphere. This is why our hospital treatment program would not allow the recovering adolescent to return to a dysfunctional system if not in treatment. We arranged for a recovering family to become surrogate or foster parents until the biological family or guardians consented to treatment. When chemically dependent adults were unable to obtain family/significant others in their treatment, we asked them to identify someone they knew or worked with to share in this process.

Addicts must have a support system and be active in a 12 Step program beyond their peers. Peer groups are essential, but networks with a church, Bible study groups, weekly support groups, or work support groups, as well as and activities with new friends who provide sustenance, are necessary.

Those who have been affected by addiction may take years to recover as they rebuild their lives, independent of what the addicted family member does. It can seem overwhelming, but keep in mind that commitment to the recovery process is commitment to the well-being of the whole family.

Constructive and active family engagement in the recovery process is essential if the family is to heal from the destructive impact of addiction. National Council on Alcoholism and Drug Dependency asserts:

"Fathers, mothers, single parents, couples straight or gay, regardless of ethnicity or social group, rich or poor...drug and alcohol abuse can destroy relationships. Most of all, young children and adolescents suffer the greatest from the effects of the abuse of alcohol and drugs in the family. But, with help and recovery, both for the individual and the family, families can heal together." [29]

CHAPTER 6

COUNSELING FOR CHANGE

I previously discussed the myth of the "magic wand," and reminded you do not have one. There is no "silver bullet" for solving your client's CD. Counseling is a powerful process for guiding, educating, confronting, and disclosing the dynamics of CD. Your responsibility is not to provide gifts of recovery but to help your client unwrap the gifts available within. Here are some more effective tools from the contributions of NLP.

REFRAMING

I have reviewed the method for eliciting your client's values and beliefs. I remind you that the technique is for uncovering behaviors, values, and beliefs in relation to your client's positive intentions. You are not to change anything. This chapter introduces a proven method for guiding change in your client called reframing.

Reframing is the process of changing or altering the frame of reference used in perceiving an experience or situation. There are two ways to guide someone in reframing an incident: six-step reframing and content reframing.

Six-Step Reframing

This model seeks to figure out the positive intention of a behavior and create optional behaviors to satisfy that intention. Have your client associate his behaviors to his drinking and drugging. (You will notice that the first three steps are similar to the explanation in chapter 3.)[30]

1. Ask your client to identify an unwanted or troubling behavior when he's been drinking or using. Make sure that he is specific.

2. Request that he contact the part of him that generates this behavior. Help him to amplify this process by probing for pictures, feelings, sounds, smells, and words associated with the behavior.

3. Help him find the positive intent of his behavior. Have your client ask the part of him initiating the behavior (which could be called the Actor), "What are you trying to do *for* me?" It is important to recognize the difference between the unwanted behavior and the positive intent motivating it. If his first response suggests a negative intent, have him ask, "What are you trying to do for me by..." (pushing me, etc.)? Continue this process until a positive intention surfaces.

4. Direct your client to access his creative part (perhaps it could be named the Creator). If he is unable to acknowledge this portion of his personality, have him imagine someone whom he believes is creative. Encourage him to form an image of this individual. You want him to contact the Creator in himself or another and request, "Please give me three alternative ways that I can get my intended outcome without drinking or using."

5. When three new behaviors or actions are presented, have him recall the Creator who launched the undesirable behavior. The Creator is to ask the Actor if he will accept responsibility for the new choices. If the answer is yes, continue. "Will you be responsible for initiating one of these new options whenever it's appropriate?" If the answer is no, guide your client back to step four and proceed.

6. The final step is known as an "ecological check." Invite your client to go inside mentally and check with any part (Creator, Actor, etc.) that might object to what has been negotiated. Pause and ask, "Is there any part of you refusing to accept the new behavior(s)?" If the answer is yes, return to step two and continue. If the answer is no, you have completed the reframe process.

Content Reframing

This mode of reframing requires you know the distinct content of the client's situation before prompting the reframing process. There are two types of content reframes: context and meaning.

Context Reframing

Context reframing means changing the setting or environment to one where the behavior is more appropriate. *Caution!* This reframe step should not be used with a chemically dependent client in relation to modifying drinking or using patterns. Abstinence is the primary goal for any addicted person.

Context reframing is helpful to the CD client in terms of other issues such as interpersonal concerns. Some behaviors are not appropriate, and these would be dealt with through the six-step reframing method.

The Process

1. Ask your client, "What is it that you want to stop or change?" Restate what he says as you understand the answer. Continue only after there is mutual agreement.

2. Ask him, "I want you to approach the Creator within you and ask, 'Is there some place in your life where this behavior is or could be useful and appropriate?'"

3. If the answer is yes, say, "Go inside, and ask the Actor part of you, who originates this behavior, if he would be willing to generate this behavior only in that context."

4. If the answer is no, say, "I want you to recall a situation where you experienced this unwanted behavior. Now make contact with the Creator part of you, and have him change the background, not the behavior, until you find one that is appropriate. Keep substituting the background until you find one that is useful. When you have found a suitable context, let your Creator share this setting with the Actor in you. Ask the Actor if he is willing to use this behavior only in this context." An answer of yes brings the reframe to closure; an answer of no returns you to the step immediately before.

It is valuable to enhance this process by encouraging your client to use all his senses: feeling, hearing, seeing, etc. Make sure that he is congruent with his words, feelings, gestures, and behavior when the reframe is finally stated. Otherwise, the reframe will not be successful.

Meaning Reframing

This process is for changing the intention or stimulus for the behavior, not the behavior itself. Meaning reframing involves altering a perception about your behavior/experience or that of another person. Sometimes it is beneficial to imagine the positive intentions of a significant other. You can learn to stop the frustration or minimize it by understanding the meaning behind the behavior.

The Process

1. Ask your client to state a complaint or problem regarding a behavior or experience regarding him or another.

2. Say to him, "Create an internal image or thought of the complaint or problem. Feel what it is like, describe what you see and hear, etc."

3. Ask him: "What does this behavior or experience *mean* to you? Has there ever been a time that it meant something different to you?"

4. If the answer is no, ask him, "What else could this behavior or experience mean?" Have your client continue to probe for a positive meaning to the behavior or situation until one is identified.

5. Ask him, "Describe the situation again with your new understanding or meaning. Are you satisfied with your understanding?" An affirmative reply indicates a successful reframe.

If the client is having difficulty finding a new frame by your pacing and leading, consider a reframe that you think will get an affirmative response.

Have your client repeat the complaint, and deliver your reframe. For example, if the client says, "No one in my family gives me any support. I always have to do things for others," your reframe could be, "I appreciate seeing someone who has a commitment to his family."

Watch for nonverbal changes when your client considers what you have said. If the reframe is productive, you will observe him transition from complaining about the problem to some acceptance of the value of what he is doing or at least seeing it within a different frame of reference.

Reframing is a good tool. It is composed of both simple and complex dynamics, and there are numerous factors to be considered when determining the success of a reframe. The analogical elements, within the client's autonomic nervous system (acts as the control center for heart rate, digestion, respiratory rate, etc.) will give you observable signs when a reframe is working. You will see elevated muscle tension and increased blood flow. The skin whitens as the blood vessels and pupils constrict. Normally this activity in the sympathetic nervous system (prepares the body to react to stress, emergency or danger) and is generated when the client is identifying and describing the problem or considering the change resulting from a reframe.

You will see when your client has gotten the desired resolution because you witness his muscles relax, skin flush, and blood vessels and pupils expand. His words, voice tone, and behavior are congruent. When this happens, the reframe is fully integrated.

The meaning reframe method is usually a quick operation. Your client does not realize the significance of what is happening other than that the complaint or problem seems momentarily resolved.

The following exercise gives you a chance to explore any personal behaviors you perceive as unpleasant. Use one or both reframing methods to examine one or more of these behaviors and see what you discover.

Personal Reframing Exercise

1. Identify three behaviors that give you concern.

2. Choose one of these behaviors, and use the six-step reframing method to discover new behavioral options. When you have satisfactorily finished the reframe, write down the three behaviors you selected.

3. Choose another unwanted behavior, and use the content reframing model. (You may want to specify a specific problem or complaint that you have with the behavior.) Try context reframing first, and find out if your problem behavior is more suitable in another setting. If so, take a moment to write down the appropriate context.

4. If you do not have a context reframe, go to the meaning reframing, and consider whether a new meaning or understanding could be made regarding the behavior. When completed, write down the new meaning. If you discover more than one meaning, choose the one that seems more relevant.

FUTURE PACING

Future pacing is a method for directing your client into a projected future and imagining how to transform his new behaviors and beliefs into desired outcomes without the use of chemicals.

It is a way of rehearsing changes and anchoring them in a new or updated belief system in abstinence, sobriety, and recovery.

Future pacing is typically an additional step in the reframing process. I have found this an effective way of developing your client's anti-sabotage plan as a part of relapse prevention. Terence Gorski, a leading author and trainer on relapse prevention, claims, "Relapse can be prevented. It's as easy as adding some special skills to the <u>recovery tool</u> kit."

Whenever you are counseling your client using any of the methods presented here, please be sensitive to timing, and allow sufficient intervals between each question. Don't hurry through any step.

The Process

It is best to have your client write down or verbally identify old behaviors and circumstances when he was using or drinking. These need to include "slippery" (relapse-prone) people, places, and things. This is a good homework assignment for the next session. Emphasize the using behaviors more than the people and places. Have him bring the written homework to the next session.

1. Begin pacing your client by suggesting, "Imagine yourself in the future in a place or situation where you have exhibited one of your old behaviors."

2. Say, "Now let a picture or image take shape in your mind so that you can experience being there. You have available new resources for coping with this situation.

Choose one of your new options, and apply it now. Let yourself experience what it is like having fresh choices. Be aware of what you are seeing, hearing, and feeling."

3. Continue prompting by saying, "If the option you selected does not fit or feels unsuitable now, choose another new behavior that you have learned. Again, focus on what you are feeling, hearing, and seeing in the old environment with newfound skills."

4. Make certain that your client experiences the power of these new options and the means for enacting them. If he has difficulty during the future pacing, take some time to explore what old feelings, beliefs, and values may be intruding. Give permission and protection to your client in using his new choices.

If your client finds it arduous to discharge new alternative behaviors or beliefs, return to the ecological check in the reframing strategy, and explore where the resistance exists. Help your client to examine other behavioral options that are acceptable to him. Once this is done, you can return to future pacing.

Future pacing can be applied to any situation or relationship, and it is effective in evaluating the success of the various reframing methods. There is an advantage in future pacing encounters a client could have with a significant others. He can deal with his anticipation of family or marital sessions, homework assignments, or any event where new options will be used.

Three Interaction Dynamics

Three types of communication most commonly used in counseling, especially group counseling, are confrontation, leveling, and feedback. These are not synonymous, and clear application of these dynamics will enhance interpersonal effectiveness. They are to be employed in appropriate ways when teaching your clients effective ways of communicating. The dynamics are defined below with clarifying examples. Practice them with friends, peers, and clients every day.

Confrontation

Confrontation is when I share how I experience or perceive your behaviors, attitudes, feelings, etc.; it is my response to what you say or do. Confronting someone is for the confronter and not the one being confronted. Confrontation is done with firmness and kindness, and it never takes away anyone's rights and dignity. Here are a few examples:

"I feel you are withdrawing from me when you sit and say nothing."

"I get angry with you when you interrupt me before I am through talking."

"I feel a sense of warmth and closeness to you when you smile."

Leveling

Leveling is disclosing how I feel when you confront me, or it can be taking a risk to share with you through my initiative. Some people want to level with a verbal attack. They have earned a "black belt" in *Verbate* (rhymes with "karate") which is using words psychologically and emotionally to devastate another. This is not leveling, and it does little to keep the channels of communication open. Leveling is not counter-confrontation; this is typically referred to as "dumping" through emotional exploitation.

When you are leveling with someone, you are stating sincerely what you are experiencing. It may or may not be a general comment, specifically addressed to anyone. Leveling in this way is an active rather than reactive dynamic. An example is when I share with you, "I am excited about writing this book and apprehensive about what value it will have for you." Other examples include the following:

"I get angry when you tell me things that I have done that are upsetting you."

"I appreciate your honesty, even though I am feeling threatened now."

"I feel excited when I am given an opportunity to learn something new about myself."

Feedback

Feedback is any type of observable (not subjective) data that can be helpful to an individual in assessing or changing a behavior, belief, or attitude. Feedback is for you (the receiver) and not me (the sender). You must be available and willing to listen to what is given; otherwise, this is another way for me to continue "dumping" on you.

As a counselor, you will have many insights and observations that could be helpful to a client. The time and place for disclosing this information is pivotal. If your client is not accessible mentally and emotionally, your feedback will be ignored, discounted, or sensed as criticism.

I never offer feedback to a client without asking for his permission to receive it, and I do not even make the request when I am uncertain how beneficial my feedback will be. Never give feedback if someone does not consent to it; to do so is psycho-emotional abuse.

You may be wondering what is done with the addicted client whose denial system is so rigid that he continuously refuses feedback. Confrontation or leveling is appropriate in this instance. Teaching significant others and group members these skills must be done before allowing them to engage in breaking through denial. You will need to model these communication styles throughout your sessions with clients, because few of them know how to talk with clarity and directness. The following feedback patterns are constructive and timely:

"Tom, when Susan was giving you a compliment, I noticed that you began to laugh and quickly changed the topic."

"Are you aware that each time you talk about your mother you clench your fist?"

Note that the feedback does not judge, analyze, or interpret the behavior. This is information for the client to check out and decide its relevance or meaning.

Teaching clients healthy techniques for productive communication could well be the best tool a counselor can offer. Whenever you encounter a client or therapy group (or anyone, for that matter), stay alert to your communication patterns.

REVIEW OF COMMUNICATION PATTERNS

1. Write down an example of a time that you confronted someone. What did you say? How did you say it?

2. Reflecting on this incident, did you use the confrontation pattern effectively? If so, congratulations! If not, how could you have improved your communication?

3. Recall and write about a situation in which you leveled with a person or group. Were you initiating your response or reacting to another person's confrontation or feedback? What would you do differently?

4. Have you recently given or received feedback? In reviewing what you said or heard, would you consider it appropriate feedback? If not, how was it inappropriate?

Conclusion

Let me underscore the importance of the ongoing development of your counseling and therapy skills. People are seldom over trained or so knowledgeable that they have no need for updating and improving their professional competence. The field of addictions is changing too fast, and health-care services are continually redesigned. Health-care providers are mandated to improve their quality of care.

The objectives presented in this book are guidelines and need to be adapted to your style and personality. These are directions, not maps to be rigidly travelled. They are methods to guide your counseling, not formulas for predetermined results.

Build **rapport** in your first session, and everything else will fall in place.

Know your **limits** and decide on your **boundaries** with your client. Know how far to go and when to stop. Admit when you are outside of your domain. Failure to do this leads to exploitation and abuse.

Exercise your powers of **potency, permission,** and **protection** each time you encounter a client. These provide the nurturing care that is indispensable to your client's fruitful recovery.

Establish therapeutic contracts regarding **escape hatches** with every client. These will need to be checked periodically during treatment and updated as needed.

Assist your client in recapturing the events, experiences, feelings, and behaviors related to his chemical use. All your counseling energy and treatment goals revolve around the current issues of his drinking or using. Addiction counseling keeps the addict's personal and interpersonal problems centered on the pathological outcomes of chemical use and abuse.

Assess and assimilate the **positive intent** relative to your client's drinking or using history. You want to affirm any positive desire behind his use without condoning the unhealthy behaviors.

Help your client correlate the consequences of his drinking or using to personal **values** and **beliefs**. The commitment to abstinence, and subsequently to sobriety and recovery, shows how well an addict connects his addiction with repeated violations of his personal values and beliefs.

Employ legitimate **leverage** for generating the client's motivation to stay in counseling or continue on the path to sobriety. The early stage of treatment rarely finds an internally motivated addict who wants to stop drinking or using. Normally, external factors predicate the decision to go into or remain in counseling. Behind any effective leverage is a value or belief that is being fulfilled by agreeing to continue the treatment process. Initially, the client experiences this as manipulation and being controlled, but the reality is that he is making a choice outside his awareness.

Model for your client healthy options for coping with distress, expressing feelings, and communicating appropriately with **confrontation, leveling,** and **feedback**. Provide him the opportunity to encounter someone who can risk, be authentic, and be accepting but does not allow conning and manipulation to continue.

You are a **conduit for change** in helping a client tap into the energy of his personal and transpersonal resources for making desired changes. The fundamental principle is to discover and accept the difference between **control** and **power; responsibility** and **surrender; sobriety** and **abstinence.**

Care for yourself, and in so doing, you ultimately care for the client. Giving away your power and energy in no way benefits your client and may be an extension of his adeptness at using others in the same way he uses a drug.

Choosing to be in a helping profession is making the decision to risk. The challenge to allow others to be vulnerable in your presence is a summons for self-disclosure. The late Sidney Jourard was a promoter for self-disclosure between a counselor and a client. He contended that counselors are to be "professional lovers," providing the healthy nurturing and protection that a patient or client seldom experiences. The healthy love you can share with your clients may not always be appreciated or understood; learn to accept that your only compensation is the fulfillment of counseling. Give up your expectation of needing results from those you counsel as a standard for personal success and competence. You may observe the changes in the lives of those you serve, but this is serendipity, a by-product of your caring and sharing. The seeds of change you plant will most likely come to fruition when your client is no longer coming to you.

It has been said that "the reward for caring is caring." I would paraphrase "the reward for counseling is counseling." You are equipped with effective tools to appreciate the reward of counseling. When you use proven methods your outcomes are more successful. Your clients will be grateful to you for helping them discover their gifts of recovery. They will have self-confidence to follow the path of abstinence, sobriety, and recovery. You have taught them how to use these tools and how to apply them in their daily lives. Nothing can be more rewarding.

NOTES

[1] Voltaire, BrainyQuote.com, http:// www.brainyquote.com/quotes/ authors/v/ voltaire.html.

[2] Richard Bandler, *Using Your Brain for a Change* (Moab, UT: Real People Press, 1985), 95.

[3] Stephen Covey, *The 7 Habits of Highly Effective People: Powerful WLessons in Personal Change* (New York: Free Press, 2004), 17.

[4] Ian Stewart and Vann Joines, *TA Today: Introduction to Transactional Analysis,* 2d ed. (Chapel Hill, NC: LifeSpace Publishing), 1–61.

[5] Jean Houston, *The Possible Human: A Course in Enhancing Your Physical, Mental, and Creative Abilities* (New York: Jeremy P. Tarcher/Putnam, 1982), 2.

[6] "The Great Hippocrates, Father of (Modern) Medicine," Optimal Health Systems, http://www.Optimal healthsystems.com/ shownews.asp?id=187.

[7] "A Critical Review of Treatment Approaches for Alcohol and Drug Problems," Cian Kerrisk, Synthesis Therapy and Counselling Services, http://www.synthesis therapy.com/aod-treatment-review.php.

[8] Katherine van Wormer and Diane Rae Davis, *Addiction Treatment: A Strengths Perspective*, 3d ed. (Belmont, CA: Brooks/Cole, 2013), 13.

[9] "DSM-5 Changes: Addiction, Substance-Related Disorders and Alcoholism," John Grohol, PsychCentral Professional, http://pro.psychcentral.com/2013/dsm-5-changes-addiction-substance-related-disorders-alcoholism/004370.html.

[10] "Substance Abuse Treatment Planning," Treatment Improvement Protocol (TIP) Series, no. 44, Center for Substance Abuse Treatment, Substance Abuse and Mental Health Services Administration, http://www.ncbi.nlm.nih.gov/books/NBK64138.

[11] "Psychotherapy and the Treatment of Alcohol Dependence," Information about Alcohol and Medicine, AlcoholMD.com, http://www.alcoholmd.com/psychotherapy.htm.

[12] "Substance Use Disorder Diagnostic Schedule-5," Evince Clinical Assessments, http://www.evinceassessment.com/SUDDS-5.pdf.

[13] Richard Bandler and John Grinder, "Content Reframing: Meaning and Context" in *Reframing: Neuro-Linguistic Programming and the Transformation of Meaning* (Moab, UT: Real People Press, 1982), 5–43.

[14] "Core Concepts of a Stroke-Centered Transactional Analysis," Claude Steiner, Claude Steiner.com,.

[15] Ian Stewart, *Making Contracts for Change*, 3d ed. (Thousand Oaks, CA: Sage Publications, 2007), 119ff.

[16] Muriel James, *Breaking Free: Self-Reparenting for a New Life* (Boston: Addison-Wesley Publishing, 1981), 174.

[17] Eric Berne, *Games People Play: The Basic Handbook of Transactional Analysis* (New York: Ballantine Books, 1998).

[18] Graeme Summers and Keith Tudor, "Co-creative Transactional Analysis," *Transactional Analysis Journal* 30, no. 1 (January 2000).

[19] Ian Stewart, "The 'Three Ways Out': Escape Hatches," in *Life Scripts: A Transactional Analysis of Unconscious Relational Patterns*, ed. Richard G. Erskine (London: Karmac Books, 2010), 151–178.

[20] "Behind Every Behavior Is a Positive Intention," John David Hoag, NLPLS.com, http://www.nlpls.com/articles/positive Intent.php.

[21] "Why Are Your Values and Beliefs Important?" Rocket Coaching, rocketcoaching.wordpress.com/2011/01/16/why-are-your-values-and-beliefs-important.

[22] "Using Leverage in Counseling the Court-Referred Client, Part 1," C. Scott McMillin, RecoverySI, http://treatmentand recoverysystems.com/library/using-leverage-in-counseling-the-court-referred-client-part-1.

[23] John Wallace, "Critical Issues in Alcoholism Therapy," in *Practical Approaches to Alcoholism Psychotherapy* (New York: Plenum Press, 1985), 37–48.

[24] "Carl Rogers," Saul McLeod, Simply Psychology, http://www.simply psychology.org/carl-rogers.html.

[25] Judith Marks Mishne, *Clinical Work with Adolescents* (New York: Free Press, 1986), 11.

[26] Staci Leon Morris and Eric F. Wagner, "Adolescent Substance Use: Developmental Considerations," Florida Certification Board/ Southern Coast ATTC Monograph Series 1, http://www.attcnetwork. org/regcenters/ productDocs/14/Adolescent_Monograph_1.pdf.

[27] James G. Chan, "An Examination of Family-Involved Approaches to Alcoholism Treatment," *Family Journal* 11 (2003): 129–138.

[28] Bill Wilson, *As Bill Sees It: The AA Way of Life* (New York, NY: Alcoholics Anonymous World Services, 1967), 197.

[29] "Alcohol and Drug Abuse Affects Everyone in the Family," National Council on Alcoholism and Drug Dependence, http:// www.ncadd.org/index.php/get-help/family-information- and-education/144-family-education.

[30] Richard Bandler and John Grinder, "Reframing Dissociated States: Alcoholism, Drug Abuse, Etc.," in *Reframing: Neuro-Linguistic Programming and the Transformation of Meaning* (Moab, UT: Real People Press, 1982), 179–207.

BIBLIOGRAPHY

Barsumian, Jane. *Necessary Steps: A Family's Journey: A Family Struggles with Adolescent Addiction.* Bloomington, IN: AuthorHouse, 2004.

Black, Claudia, PhD. *Family Strategies: Practical Tools for Professionals Training Families Impacted by Addiction.* San Francisco: Mac Publishing, 2006.

Blackerby, Don A., PhD. *Rediscover the Joy of Learning.* Oklahoma City, OK: Success Skills, 1996.

Bradshaw, John. *The Family: A Revolutionary Way of Self-Discovery.* Deerfield Beach, FL: Health Communications, 1988.

Brown, Stephanie and Virginia Lewis. *Alcoholic Families in Recovery.* New York: Guilford Press, 1999.

Cook, Linda S. "Adolescent Addiction and Delinquency in the Family System." *Issues in Mental Health Nursing* 22, no. 2 (2001): 151–157.

Edwards, John T. *Treating Chemically Dependent Families: A Practical Approach for Professionals.* Center City, MN: Hazelden, 1990.

Fossum, Merle and Marilyn J. *Facing Shame: Families in Recovery.* New York, NY: W. W. Norton, 1986.

Jourard, Sidney. *The Transparent Self.* New York: S. Van Norstand, 1964.

Lewis, Bryon A. and R. Frank Pucelik. *Magic of NLP Demystified.* Williston, VT: Crown House Publishing, 2012.

Maslow, Abraham. *Toward a Psychology of Being,* 3d Ed. New York: John Wiley & Sons, 1998.

Nicholas, Mary W. *Change in the Context of Group Therapy.* New York: Brunner/Mazel Publishing, 1984.

O'Conner, Joseph and John Seymour. *Introducing NLP: Psychological Skills for Understanding and Influencing People.* San Francisco: Conari Press, 2011.

Steiner, Claude. *Scripts People Live: Transactional Analysis of Life Scripts,* 2d Ed. New York: Grove Press, 1990.

Steinglass, Peter. *The Alcoholic Family.* New York: Basic Books, 1987.

Tillich, Paul. *The Courage to Be.* New Haven, CT: Yale University Press, 1952.

Titelman, Peter, Ed. *The Therapist's Own Family.* New York, NY: Jason Aronson, 1987.

Wilson, Bill and Bob Smith. *The Big Book of Alcoholics Anonymous.* New York, NY: World Service, 2013.

ABOUT THE AUTHOR

H. Leroy Thompson is an undergraduate of Oklahoma City University and a *cum laude* graduate of Emory University, Atlanta, Georgia. He is an ordained clergyman in the United Methodist Church.

His background as a pastoral counselor includes ten years in an inner-city social action ministry working with homeless and poverty-level families. This population faced constant issues with alcoholism and drug addiction. A state mental health hospital established an outpatient "social detox" and rehab center in an adjoining building. Thompson provided volunteer services, facilitated support groups, lectured, and helped clients complete their fifth step of AA/NA.

In 1982, he joined the staff of a hospital-based CDU. Following his first position as an outpatient family counselor, he became the director of outpatient services, the clinical director of the inpatient unit, and eventually the executive director.

He trained at the Johnson Institute using the "Minnesota Model" of CD treatment developed by Hazelden, Southwest Institute of Alcohol and Chemical Dependency Studies, the Midwest Institute for Transactional Analysis, and the Oklahoma

Drug and Alcohol Professional Counselors Association. He became a certified CD counselor at the state, national, and international levels, a member of the Oklahoma Association on Alcoholism and Drug Abuse (OAADA), and a member of the Oklahoma Drug and Alcohol Professional Counselors Association (ODAPCA). He was a codeveloper, codirector, and presenter for the Summer School on Chemical Dependency at Oklahoma City University for more than twenty years. The school is currently in its thirty-second year of training clergy, professional counselors, laity, and denominational leaders from across the United States and abroad.

He became the vice president of university-church relations at his *alma mater*, Oklahoma City University. One of his duties was to provide counseling to the administration, staff, faculty, and students. He also assisted in the student drug-prevention program.

He retired from OCU in 2004. He and his wife, Sharon, reside in Edmond, Oklahoma, where they enjoy their family and friends, especially Jazzi, their Boston terrier.

READER NOTES

CPSIA information can be obtained at www.ICGtesting.com
Printed in the USA
LVOW08s1632130715

446030LV00003B/680/P

9 781494 777487